Cooking All Over the World

Shannon Bennett is the award-winning head chef of Melbourne's Vue de Monde restaurant, as well as several other venues in Melbourne, and the author of six previous cookbooks. He is a brand ambassador for Miele.

Cooking All
Over the World

Shannon Bennett

Photography by Simon Griffiths

Miele

Prologue

I'm at the airport, worrying about the fact that I've forgotten to buy my wife a birthday present, and wondering: what on earth am I doing? Somehow, I've managed to agree to travel through nineteen countries in seventy days, cooking for some of the most successful, interesting and culturally diverse people in the world. And all for an oven! Sure, it is not just any oven. The Miele Generation 6000 is probably the most technologically advanced oven ever built for the residential home market. It proves bread, for goodness' sake, and even dehydrates vegetable shavings into chips when you touch an LED screen.

It all started when Dr Markus Miele and Dr Reinhard Zinkann, joint managing directors and co-owners of the company, along with Dr Heiner Olbrich, board member and global director of sales and marketing, asked me to a casual dinner in late 2012 to discuss ways to attract a younger audience to and involve them with the Miele brand. Heiner was concerned that it was not held in high enough regard by successful young professionals.

Michael Jeanes, managing director of Miele, Australia and I explained to our German colleagues that young professionals in Australia already aspire to own Miele kitchen appliances; they perceive the brand as innovative, modern and surprising and he should not be concerned. But it turns out Dr Olbrich was referring to the rest of the world. He wanted me to take what I've been doing in Australia and take it around the world – developing recipes, training and inspiring local home economists, and teaching avid Miele customers the passion needed to find great ingredients.

Dr Zinkann said, 'Shannon, we should do a book. I want to do this with you. We have to include my vintage car rally next June. I have the perfect car for you. Madeleine and the children have to come as well.'

Dr Olbrich began to choke on his freshwater crayfish tail with tarragon butter, brought in on a hot rock. He seemed to be in shock, but then he quickly revived and took control of the conversation. He was thinking and the table fell silent.

Dr Zinkann was oblivious to the storm he'd created and continued to eat his crayfish with his fingers, as instructed by me earlier. Then Dr Olbrich cleared his throat. The next part of the conversation changed the look on Michael's face for the next twelve months, possibly forever: 'Shannon, why not travel around with us and write a travel cookbook encompassing your relationship with Miele?' There was no time to answer, but I don't think it was a question. Anyway, Dr Olbrich replied for me: 'Let's make this book fantastic, something all our customers would love to read and cook out of, something that will help us relate to our younger customers.'

'Michael, you can co-ordinate this please,' Dr Olbrich added. 'In fact, Michael, you can travel with Shannon and make sure he gets everything he needs.'

Now Michael started choking on his crayfish tail, quite violently. Amongst the splutters and coughing, he asked: 'Shannon, when can you start?'

Once again, now I'm starting to get to know Dr Olbrich, I don't think it was a question, either. I finally got a word in while Michael started to gather his thoughts: 'You mean, you would like us to conduct a visit to key European cities and their Miele Galleries to help promote the release of the new Generation 6000 oven series and write a recipe book? That all sounds very exciting, Heiner.' A 'Yes, for sure, sounds great, Dr Zinkann' flowed out of my mouth without me thinking.

The rest of the night became a creative discussion that Dr Zinkann took over with wild ideas of driving vintage cars through different cities, and having me cook dinners with and for famous politicians, artists and actors in their multi-million-dollar mansions and penthouses. 'Scott Murray, the writer, has to be involved,' I say. 'Sure, no problem, Shannon; whatever you need will be provided,' Heiner said. 'Make sure you bring the family, too,' Dr Zinkann added.

Six months later, no family, the deadline for the manuscript blown out by months and astronomical budgets in place, I think to myself, 'Well, I'm here now, so let's make the most of it.' Writing is therapy, they say. So here goes.

Departure

And now here I am at Tullamarine airport, waiting to board. Chris, my head chef, and Dan, my pastry chef, have left Melbourne twenty-four hours ahead of the photographer Simon Griffiths and me. Getting all this organised has been tough. Michael Jeanes is no fool, though, and has wisely delegated his wife Patricia to help co-ordinate the first leg of the tour, as she is already in Europe spending some time at their home in the UK. Over many years, she has developed great contacts with the Miele subsidiaries we are visiting and is about to put those relationships to good use. To her long list of organisational qualities, she now knows more about where to buy kangaroo, how to import – or sometimes smuggle – wine into every port around the world, Vue de Monde's table-setting standards, the prices of airfares and the definition of what a boutique hotel is than her husband does about electrical-compliance certificates and retail-market trends. Emails have been flying in from all around the world, sometimes fifty a day, mostly with problems rather than solutions and Patricia has become the problem-solver communicating with Australia through my assistant, Jess Peacock and Michael's executive assistant, Fiona Hastings. To be fair, this has been thrust upon every country in a very rapid way. And while not everybody is fully ready for us to descend on the doorstop of their Miele Gallery, the plane is at the gate and I am about to board.

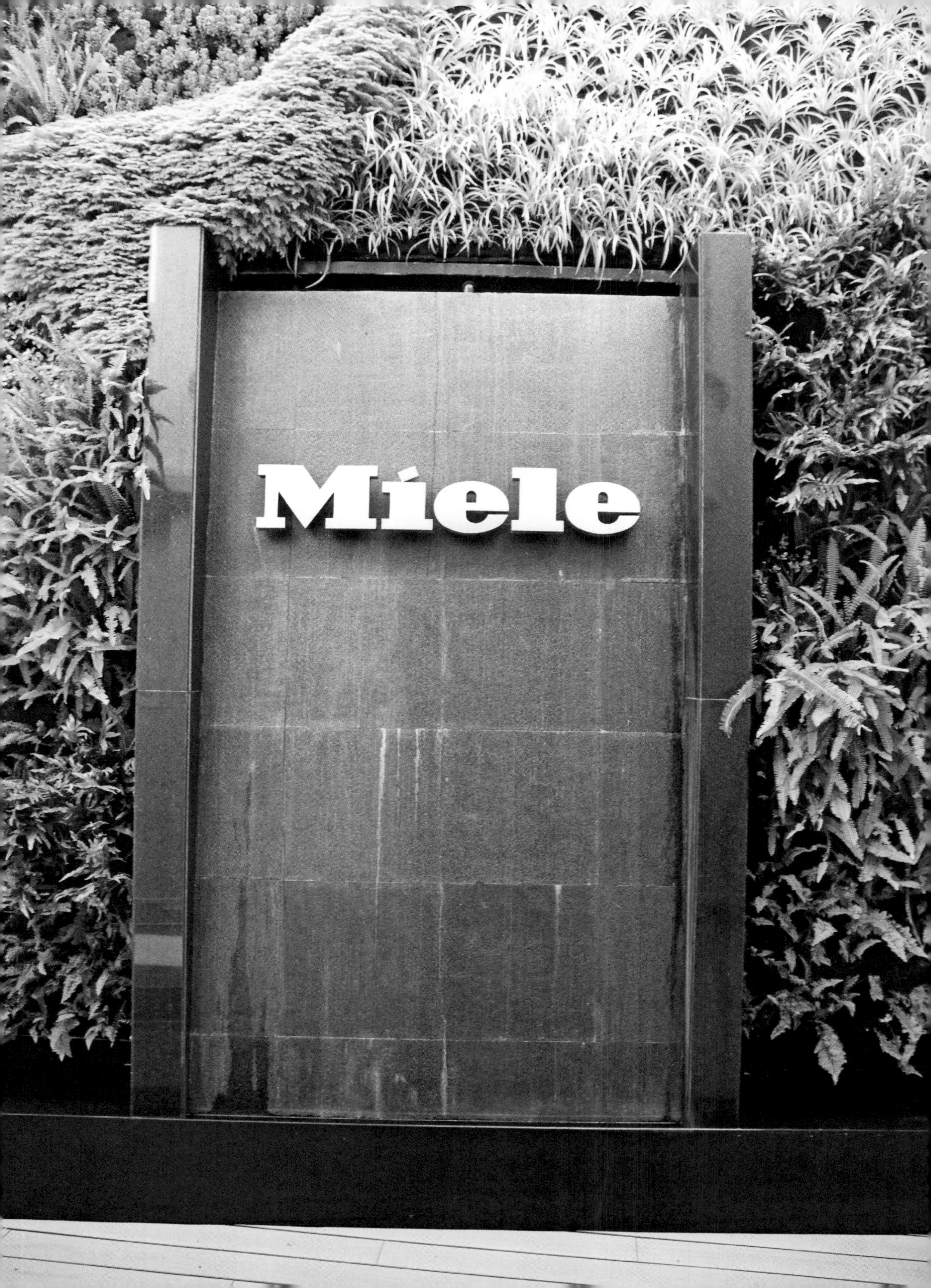
Miele

The Miele dinner

In each city I visited, I cooked a dinner for the local Miele team and other people prominent in the food scene of that city. The menu was the same each time – barramundi with prawns, kangaroo fillet, and pavlova and lamingtons for dessert. As you can tell, I wanted to give them a taste of modern Australian cuisine and ingredients, while showcasing the Miele equipment. Getting the ingredients into each country presented a challenge at times, but the results were worth it. Below I've described a few of the most memorable events, from improvising when the ingredients don't turn up, to cooking during an earthquake.

Prague

Our first launch night of the Miele Generation 6000 oven is thrust upon us. My head chefs Chris and Dan have busted their guts to get us over the line with prep. There is a lot of nervousness and anticipation as I arrive in the Miele Gallery. These guys are used to selling vacuum cleaners and washing machines, not setting up a pop-up restaurant with barramundi and kangaroo on the menu.

The event begins with guests being offered a glass of sparkling wine from Heemskerk in Tasmania's Coal River Valley, accompanied by amuse-bouches of smoked eel in white chocolate and Australian Angasi oysters.

I explain to the assembled guests that what they are about to eat is a sample of the food at my restaurant. The first course combines barramundi with smoked river prawns, accompanied by a cone of potato and a sauce made from nettles picked that morning. This is followed by roasted fillet of kangaroo combined with saltbush, roasted pears and a mustard mayonnaise.

The dessert is my deconstructed version of a pavlova, and to finish is my version of the classic Australian lamington, as well as white chocolate seashells filled with olive oil and seaweed.

The menu is a real taste of Australia, and so are the wines: a Heemskerk riesling and a pinot noir from Coldstream Hills in Victoria's Yarra Valley.

It goes off without a hitch. When I ask what people most enjoyed, the kangaroo pops up as the favourite, along with the lamingtons.

Amsterdam

We have heard a lot about the Miele Inspirience Center in Amsterdam; it is legendary amongst Miele executives as the most extravagant and impressive brand experience in the Miele world. When we arrive we understand why: there's a 100-seat restaurant, two lecture theatres, and – most incredibly – a water-tasting room that houses more than 200 waters from around the world and can take you through a round of tests to work out which water suits your palate! The team and I are greeted by a full professional brigade. By late morning, we have the dinner ready for service that night.

Guests at the dinner come from a variety of backgrounds; for instance, I meet a Dutch olive oil producer who lives in Holland most of the year but has a large plot of olives back in Tuscany. We serve her oil on the night in the white chocolate seashell with seaweed, to her surprise. Other interesting people I meet are Juius Jaspers, the host of Dutch Top Chef, an absolute giant of a man. He is a barbecue legend and extremely jovial but has a genuine passion for great food.

My good friend Hans van Manen, chairman of the Jeunes Restaurateurs d'Europe association (of which I'm fortunate to be a member), is also here. His organisation supports young restaurateurs when they start out. Talking with Hans reminds me that my work with the organisation has never really been completed, and I pledge to Hans that I will recruit some talented young chefs from Australia that the group can mentor.

Brussels

Tour & Taxis is a multi-purpose grand building, the venue for tonight's dinner. Local chef Yves Mattagne runs a cooking school and events space in this lovingly converted building opposite the canal harbour on the edge of the city centre, and has kindly loaned the space for the evening. It is decked out in all the latest and greatest Miele gear including my favourite, the wall-mounted pressure cooker/steamer. Twenty of Belgium's finest come together for us to showcase our Australian menu. The general manager for Miele Belgium makes a great speech, heaping such effusive praise on us I'm left blushing. I tell him the cheque is in the mail. The kangaroo goes down a treat and though most diners have no idea what pavlova is, they seem to enjoy it!

Istanbul

I've just done seven interviews in a jetlagged state, and walk out of the conference room on automatic pilot, telling the nearest Miele sales assistant my life story. She just looks at me strangely. My assistants look as if they have seen a ghost; I walk over to discover the butterfly effect has reared its ugly head. Batuhan, the man who has been in charge of organising our ingredients, has struggled a little. The fish that turns up is five minutes this side of rotten! The prawns are not faring much better. The chef asks for advice and I say: 'Wing it!' Going through every fridge in the Gallery, he finds a few little pickling cucumbers and some baby onions. We turn a disastrous moment into an embarrassing but bearable one. The dish is okay: prawns cooked in garlic butter with wild herbs and pickled vegetables. One thing that Turkey can improve is its butter. Generally it is not well made.

The first of the guests arrive and we are reunited with our chaperone from the previous night, Lino. With his debonair manner and youthful swagger, he is going to be the star of the night. I mention to him that we will hit the town afterwards for a 'wet burger' (a Turkish specialty); his eyes light up and he insists he will take us to the best place in town. I think I disappoint him a little when I mention that if he intends to keep me out past midnight he might need to bring a wheelbarrow because I'm so knackered I'll turn into a pumpkin.

Listing the ingredients that don't turn up is pointless; it is also pointless being angry about it. This is Istanbul. The traffic is crazy here and delays are inevitable. We manage somehow and the night concludes with the butcher, Cuneyt, stealing the show and deflecting away the dishes that were below par and incomplete with a wave of his hand. Potential shambles now turned on its head, it's time to hit the town.

Singapore

The dinner here is a more formal event than usual. Two violinists pop out from behind the kitchen playing 'Waltzing Matilda'. One, a gentleman in his sixties, is wearing a Crocodile Dundee hat and has a stuffed crocodile hanging out of his pants. Cringe! I soon find out these theatre restaurant impresarios are in fact Alexander Souptel, recently retired concertmaster of the Singapore Symphony Orchestra, and master violinist Masako Suzuki White. This is what Singapore is like – grand yet with moments of spontaneity.

Santiago

The Miele Gallery here is a real spectacle, surrounded by fashionable restaurants and boutique shops in the new Santiago. The staff are well prepared for the thirty guests who will be served their four-course meal on the rooftop of the building. I am admiring the set-up and checking some details from the roof, when dogs from surrounding houses start to bark madly. It really catches my attention. A minute later the building sways, and I haven't even had a glass of bubbly. It is an earthquake! I've never experienced one, and all sorts of emotions run through me. The shaking stops as abruptly as it starts and everyone except me and my team continues with their work. We look at each other in wobbly amazement. That was no mere earth tremor! I rush down to the lobby of the Gallery to ensure everything and everyone is okay, to find everybody still carrying on as normal. The Big Boss spots the startled Aussie in his lobby and reassures me, 'Bah! This is Chile!' Well, that's my first-ever dinner conducted during an earthquake.

Amsterdam

A city of canals and cycling,
and a search for heirloom carrots
with the purest flavour.

Amsterdam is a city of incredible originality and a type of understated class. The Dutch don't do architecture to admire; they design places to live in and they like to live in nice places. Hotel buildings don't look like hotel buildings and bars look like houses; I challenge people to find a 7-11 in this town, let alone a supermarket anywhere in the 'CBD', if you can even call it that. If you look at the structure of the city in a satellite photo, the canals shape it into a series of circles inside each other. Space is at a premium. History is not.

Dutch tradition

Holland is a province within the Netherlands, which translates as 'lowlands'. Here you can find some of the most fertile land in Europe, one of the reasons why Holland is Europe's 'head office' of agriculture.

Of course we are here to do a job for Miele, which begins tomorrow when we travel south to a small village called Vianen, where the largest Miele Center in the world is found. But my mission for today is to find the truth about the humble carrot. My research has led me to conclude the carrot originated from Afghanistan and was originally white. Records exist that suggest the Romans used the green tops of carrots, rather than the root, for medicinal purposes. Around the tenth century, the carrot was being traded in markets all over middle Asia; artwork from the era shows purple and yellow varieties. Apparently, in the early sixteenth century, Dutch farmers to the royal court were instructed to start producing orange carrots. From then on carrots as they are today became prevalent. Fascinatingly, the white and yellow carrots have the purest flavour. Surprisingly, the chefs I ask about the history of the carrot seem to be baffled by my enquiry! Maybe I am a food geek. ➔

1–2 Amsterdam's famous canals snake through the city, giving it a distinctive character. As most people travel either by bicycle or boat, the city is usually incredibly quiet.

3 Amsterdam's museum of science, the Science Center NEMO, looks like something from a science fiction movie.

The big picture starts to take shape: do the Dutch have a national food culture or is it no longer relevant? I have to confess I don't know a whole lot about Dutch food. Is pickled herring a way to sum up the cuisine in one ingredient? Most people I speak to seem to think so. I challenge Frank, my Miele guide, to dig deeper and tell me which other dishes speak Dutch to him. He answers: asparagus, baked carrots, strawberries, new potatoes and pretty much anything that comes in the form of a vegetable. I am more confused than ever and no closer to understanding the food culture here.

Frank starts to awaken to my persistent goading and becomes more expansive. 'Okay, some Danes or Germans might say, "Hey, I have eaten herrings all my life!" I say, "Yes correct, they eat herrings, but they are Dutch herrings!"' The Dutch are said to have invented the method of preserving salted herrings in wooden barrels. Their culture may not, in fact, be defined by its ingredients but by its originality. Its resourcefulness. Frank describes Dutch people as swarthy; I ask him what he means. He says 'We have the same attitude as people from the Caribbean or central Africa. We love life and we are resourceful.' I get Frank's point of view, especially after noticing a family moving into a canal-side townhouse: a small winch lifts a set of kids' bunk beds from a boat, up the side of a four-storey building and through a large window. The captain of the boat tells me that this is the way all furniture is moved for canal-side houses and flats.

'*Doenormaal,*' Frank says. It means 'act normal', 'feel free' or 'do what you like', and Frank believes that this is one of the national characteristics of the Dutch; a relaxed attitude is seen as important to wellbeing. Probably the main reason why marijuana cafes exist in the city and drugs in general seem to be accepted as long as they do not trigger anti-social behaviour. The rest of the world may learn a little from this cultural attitude.

Indonesian food is popular and as authentic if not even more defined than in restaurants in Indonesia itself. There is literally an Indonesian restaurant on every street. You're also likely to find a bar that specialises in Geneva gin. Most Dutch drink this gin straight and to my liking they treat gin very similarly to the way the Scots drink whisky. Lucas Bols brand is the most famous. ➔

4   A statue of the Dutch philosopher Spinoza, who espoused freedom and tolerance – principles which shape the character of the city.

5   A tranquil Amsterdam scene. The following day was Gay Pride Day, transforming the canal into a parade of colour and joyful, noisy crowds.

6–7   A typical small bar serving Geneva gin.

Lindenhoff

A real Dutch farmers' market, on the site of a former coach stop from the sixteenth century. It specialises in Gascoigne cattle, a breed that has been involved in veal production for 500 years in the Netherlands. On the site now is a vegetable farm, egg farm, small piggery and public farmers' market that opens four days per week, where other local producers are encouraged to come and sell their goods from the one big old farm shed. The vegetable farm has another special story. The mechanics of the farm rely heavily on old-fashioned knowledge and hard work. The farm started a program with a local authority to employ day-release prisoners, homeless people and young people who are having problems with addiction. They are offered knowledge and jobs through well-supervised programs where they also learn about the 200 or so restaurants they supply and hopefully some find their calling and enter either the farming industry or hospitality. Several years ago the farm expanded to include a very small amount of veal and beef production. We are talking tiny. Only four cows are slaughtered a week; that is only eight fillets and eight strip loins a week, and it's the most in-demand product in the Netherlands. There is a waiting list to obtain veal from this farm.

We all know of the horror stories and barbaric practices that have been used in the veal industry. Eva, one of the managers at the farm, tells me that here, 'We produce veal that is different to what the old way was, no hormones, no cruel practices and organic philosophy with our fields.' For us even to be taken through a veal farm is a very rare thing. Dutch farmers are very aware of the negative image that veal production has. This is why Eva is so enthusiastic about showing us around, and takes us to the sheds where the young cows are free to roam and walk the fields to feed on natural grasses and weeds. The farm is only two years old and was developed in conjunction with a local university to study the viability of this method of veal production. They hope to use it as a textbook case to convince other farmers to move towards sustainable farming practices and rely far less on manufactured, grain-based animal feed. They aim to use preventative medicine rather than relying heavily on antibiotics, to move towards veal being slaughtered around the twelve-month mark, and to convince chefs that veal should be more pronounced in colour and flavour. ●

8   Tourist boats are available for sightseeing cruises along Amsterdam's famous canals.
9–12 The farmers' market. Holland has some of the most fertile land in Europe thanks to its low-lying terrain.

13–14 Sights along the canal.
15   Amsterdam is a famously cycle-friendly city; you quickly notice the number of people travelling by bike, as well as the bicycles chained to every available surface.
16   The Heineken Brewery. It was established in 1864 but now operates as a museum and beer-themed 'amusement park'.
17   The *Zuiderkerk,* or 'southern church'. This was the first Protestant church built in Amsterdam.

Herring soup

Serves 4

For me, Amsterdam's restaurant scene reflects South East Asian cuisine far more than I was expecting – Vietnamese and Indonesian food are particularly well represented. Armed with this new insight, the recipe below is a hybrid of what I would cook on a Sunday afternoon if I lived in The Netherlands, where both mussels and herrings are in plentiful supply. The soup can be served hot or chilled, and feel free to experiment by adding different herbs, vegetables and aromatics to the dish.

4 herring fillets, cleaned and cut into thirds
1 granny smith apple, cut into matchsticks
1 large beetroot, peeled and cut into matchsticks
12 small mint leaves, washed
12 small Vietnamese basil leaves, washed
puffed rice, to garnish

Mussel juice
500 g mussels, cleaned and de-bearded
400 ml white wine
100 ml water
3 sprigs thyme
1/2 golden shallot, peeled and roughly chopped

Soup
1/2 cup (60 g) mushroom stalks
1 onion, cut in half, peeled and thinly sliced
2 cloves garlic, crushed
4 slices ginger
1 stalk lemongrass, crushed and
**   roughly chopped**
1 tablespoon chopped coriander stalk
1 cup (250 ml) water
sea salt and sugar, to taste
1 cup (250 ml) coconut cream, whipped
juice of 1 lime, or to taste

To make the mussel juice, heat a large saucepan over high heat. Add the mussels, then cover with a lid so they start steaming straight away. Pour in the wine and water, then add the thyme sprigs and shallot. Bring to the boil, then reduce the heat to low and simmer, covered, for 2 minutes. Check with a toothpick or cake tester – if it goes through, the mussels are cooked. Strain, reserving the liquid. (The mussels can be eaten now if you wish.)

To make the soup, place the mushroom, onion, garlic, ginger, lemongrass and coriander stalk in a medium saucepan, cover with the water and 2 cups (500 ml) mussel juice and simmer over low heat for 45 minutes. Strain through a sieve into a clean saucepan, discarding the solids, and season to taste with salt and sugar.

Distribute the herring pieces evenly among 4 bowls and top each piece with a little apple and beetroot. Finish each little pile with the mint and basil leaves and a little puffed rice.

Just before serving, bring the soup to the boil, then reduce the heat and simmer while whisking in the coconut cream. Season to taste with lime juice.

Pour the soup carefully into each bowl at the table and serve.

Simmered veal cheeks with hete bliksem ('hot lightning')

Serves 4

Veal is a national ingredient for the Dutch. Yes, this does involve animal rights issues but as avid cooks and passionate modern-day citizens we now can ask the tough questions and ensure we always choose ethical produce. And these days there are some great producers rearing veal using ethical methods. 'Hot lightning' is also a national dish. Who can resist apples and potatoes cooked together? Many say the dish got its unusual name from the phrase 'heaven and earth' – the apples from heaven and the potatoes from the earth – while others link it to thunder and lightning. Whatever the story, the dish really does seem to retain its heat longer than conventional mashed potato! Why? No idea.

**800 g veal brisket, trimmed and cut into
   8 even pieces**
2 golden shallots, peeled and thinly sliced
4 large carrots, peeled and cut into 1 cm dice
1 small celeriac, peeled and cut into 1 cm dice
2 cloves garlic, crushed
2 star anise
1 litre chicken stock

Hete bliksem
**400 g Opperdoeser ronde or royal blue
   potatoes, peeled and cut into 2 cm dice**
**2 large elstar or red delicious apples, peeled,
   cored and cut into 2 cm dice**
**1 brown onion, cut in half, peeled and
   thinly sliced**
100 g piece smoked streaky bacon
100 g cultured butter, cut into cubes
sea salt

Preheat the oven on the conventional setting to 150°C.

Place the veal pieces, shallot, carrots, celeriac, garlic and star anise in a large ovenproof saucepan or flameproof casserole dish and cover with the chicken stock. Bring to the boil over high heat, then cover with a tight-fitting lid and place in the oven. Bake for 4 hours or until the veal is super tender.

About 40 minutes before you are ready to serve, make the hete bliksem. Place the potato in a medium saucepan and cover with cold water. Layer the apple and onion over the potato, followed by the piece of bacon. Bring to the boil over high heat and cook for about 15 minutes or until the potato is tender. Drain, then mash the potato mixture in either a mouli or food processor until it is smooth and creamy. Add the butter and season to taste with salt.

To serve, divide the heke bliksom, veal and braising juices evenly among warmed plates. Serve immediately whilst lightning hot!

Wentelteefjes

Serves 4

Chocolate plays an important role in the Dutch family diet, especially in a custard dessert called vla. Vla would not normally be served with wenteleefje (essentially French toast, the Dutch way) but I found both dishes on the same plate for my last brunch in The Netherlands and the combination of crisp spiced bread and chocolate custard took me straight back to my childhood, when calories were irrelevant! Fresh strawberries are the perfect finishing touch. By the way, strawberries should never be stored in the fridge, as the sugars go to sleep and turn the flavour sour. Keep them in a cool, dark spot in the pantry and eat them quickly.

400 ml creme anglaise
½ cup (90 g) finely chopped couverture
    chocolate (70% cocoa solids)
2 cinnamon sticks
3 star anise
125 g caster sugar
700 ml milk
2 eggs
4 × 2 cm thick slices white bread,
    crusts removed
1 tablespoon melted butter
20 strawberries, hulled and cut in half
icing sugar, for dusting

Gently warm the creme anglaise in a small saucepan over low heat (be careful not to let it boil). Add the chocolate, then remove from the heat and stir until all the chocolate has melted and the mixture is smooth. Allow to cool in the fridge.

Combine the cinnamon, star anise, sugar and milk in a medium saucepan and bring to the boil. Reduce the heat and simmer until it reduces by half. Remove and set aside to cool for 5 minutes, then strain. Whisk the eggs into the cooled milk.

Place the bread slices in the milk mixture and leave to soak for 30 seconds.

Preheat the oven on intensive grill to 160°C. Brush a baking tray with melted butter and place under the grill to heat through.

Carefully remove the bread slices from the milk and place them on the hot baking tray. Grill for 5–6 minutes each side or until they are golden brown and crisp. Allow to cool slightly.

With your fingers, rip the bread into 4–5 pieces and place them on each plate. Dust with icing sugar and serve with the chocolate custard and strawberries while the bread is still warm.

Visitor tips

Hotels

717 Hotel
Prinsengracht 717, 1017 JW
☎ **+31 20 427 0717**
717hotel.nl
This place has a very unassuming entrance.
Once you enter the small hallway with
three delightful sitting rooms, you realise
why it's so popular with those in the know.
It's full of strategically placed Dutch and
German antiques and soft 'sink into'
couches. I am quickly introduced to the
hotel duty manager, Markus, who is the
concierge and front desk supervisor plus
full-time cool local dude. 717 is the real
deal when it comes to being a boutique
hotel. Breakfast here has a touch of the
old generation about it, sitting in the
basement dining room, looking out on
to a small courtyard filled with pot plants
and overgrown creepers.

Restaurants

Restaurant As
Prinses Irenestraat 19, 1077 WT
☎ **+31 20 644 0100**
restaurantas.nl
Amsterdam's culinary wunderkinder
are a cerebral bunch and no restaurant
is more thoughtful than this one in the
South Axis district, which makes the
Slow Food movement look manic. That's
mostly because chef Sander Overeinder
likes you to see exactly where your dinner
is coming from. The largely one-man show
restricts the menu to three main courses,
but when the dishes land on the long, oak
communal tables punctuating the circular
dining room they justify the diners' almost
reverential silence.

Restaurant Bridges
Oudezijds Voorburgwal 197, 1012 EX
☎ **+31 20 555 3560**
bridgesrestaurant.nl
We didn't eat here but all the locals
raved about this place.

Restaurant Lucas Rive ↑
Oude Doelenkade 7, Hoorn,
Terschelling 1621 BH
☎ **+31 22 921 3362**
lucasrive.nl
The quaint seaside town of Hoorn is
a must for seafood-lovers and gastronomes
who want a day out of Amsterdam. Lucas
Rive and his family run one of the many
good local restaurants in the town; this
one happens to have earned two Michelin
stars. The outside terrace is the place for
lunch on a warm summer's day. There
is an a la carte and degustation menu on
offer. We are in the chef's hands and we
are not disappointed. Fresh turbot with
wild mushrooms is a highlight, and so is
fresh crab salad bound in mayonnaise
accompanied by the brown crab meat.
We have some fun in the kitchen after
lunch, plating and mucking around with
a few dishes based on local seafoods. Lucas
and his family are certainly passionate. If
you're in the area it is well worth the visit.

Auckland

A generous city, where seasonal produce
reigns and the influence of
Pacific Island culture is strong.

First stop is the French Kitchen, the private dining room of the French Cafe, for dinner, straight from the airport. This restaurant is consistently talked about as Auckland's best. Clean, superbly executed dishes that are, most importantly, local and seasonal. The room is very attractive, with mid-century and modern Danish furniture pieces. Well worth the booking for dinner here.

After a great night's sleep at Mollies (see Visitor Tips), a decent caffeine boost is imperative. My NZ mates and Cafe Vue team members tell me Cafe Espresso is one of the best coffee houses in the city. Cafe culture in this city is strong but still has a few yards to travel before it competes with Melbourne.

Food-wise, New Zealand has a very distinctive culture; Pacific Island influence runs deep in the veins of every New Zealander, regardless of their specific origin. But does it influence their everyday eating habits? I ask Michael Meredith, a local Samoan chef whom I met several years ago, what defines the food of this country. His restaurant, Merediths, is regarded as one of the best in the country, greatly influenced by Michael's proud heritage. Michael tells me, 'NZ cuisine is largely driven by seasonally grown produce, and the thriving diversity of different cultures here has given our young food its own identity and flavour.' With the kind of egalitarian generosity and patriotism I'm discovering everywhere here, he presses me to visit Masu, a restaurant that will further my understanding. Ah, the tyranny of tight schedules!

On that note, I have to press pause on my search as I'm off to help launch the new Miele Center in Freemans Bay. Michael Jeanes and the Miele team worked around the clock over three weeks to complete the Center. We have over one hundred of New Zealand's finest architects, developers, retailers and customers to feed, kicking off with a traditional Maori welcome and blessings. Provided no one in the kitchen sets fire to anything, I'm happy. ●

1–3 The French Kitchen, where we have our first meal in Auckland – an impressive introduction to the city's culinary scene.

4   The Three Lamps bar, now sadly closed, in the magnificent Ponsonby building, a former post office in the Edwardian baroque style, designed by architect John Campbell.

5   Jack Tar, a bar and cafe/eatery that opens for breakfast and stays open all day.

6   Dizengoff, a local institution.

7   Bambina cafe in Ponsonby.

8   Auckland's new Miele Center.

9   With Michael Meredith, Miele Auckland's brand ambassador.

10   The ASB North Wharf, controversial winner of New Zealand's 2014 Architecture Award, where many cafes and eateries are now located.

Grilled green-lip mussels with crayfish

Makes 10

New Zealand has some of the best seafood in the world. My two favourites are bluff oysters and green-lip mussels. I have a lot of respect for these generously fat, delicate molluscs, and because they are so cheap you've got to make the most of them. Buy an extra kilo and steam them up for no more than 2 minutes; remember to capture the juices from the steaming tray, as these can be used as the base for a sauce or dressing. Enjoy a simple dinner of steamed mussels with buttered brown bread and a glass of New Zealand riesling, and use the leftover uncooked mussels to make the recipe below.

10 green-lip mussels
½ cup (100 g) chopped cooked crayfish or lobster meat
1 heaped tablespoon roughly chopped tarragon
juice of ¼ lemon
sea salt
4 eggs, beaten
1 teaspoon dijon mustard
½ cup (125 ml) grapeseed oil
1 tablespoon seaweed, finely sliced

Preheat the steamer to 100°C. Cook the mussels for 2 minutes or until opened, then transfer them to a colander resting over a bowl and cover with plastic film. Allow to cool for 5 minutes. Pick the mussels from the shell, then check for any beard and pull away (reserve the shells). Roughly chop the mussels and mix with the crayfish or lobster meat. Add the tarragon and lemon juice and season to taste with salt.

In a medium stainless steel bowl, combine the egg, mustard and a pinch of salt. Slowly whisk in the grapeseed oil until the sauce thickens to the consistency of a light mayonnaise.

Preheat the oven on fan grill to 220°C.

Combine the sauce with the mussel mixture, then taste and add a little more salt if necessary. Divide the seaweed among half the mussel shells, and spoon the mussel mixture on top. Place the filled shells on a baking tray and grill for 2 minutes or until the mixture starts to colour slightly. Serve immediately on a platter or individual plates.

Lamb with thyme and lemon

Serves 4

New Zealand lamb is world famous; however, within the industry, local chefs eagerly await an even better quality of lamb. The best lamb is available in autumn when the pastures are at their best, the mothers are in prime condition and the milk they produce is at its most nutritious.

1 × 500 g lamb leg
1.3 litres chicken stock
90 g cultured butter
1 golden shallot, peeled, cut in half and
**   finely chopped**
1 tablespoon finely chopped flat-leaf parsley
sea salt
finely grated zest and juice of ½ lemon
8 savoy cabbage leaves, central stem removed
iced water
1 tablespoon olive oil
2 × 150 g young lamb loins
2 sprigs young thyme, plus extra to garnish

Preheat the oven on the conventional setting to 140°C.

Place the lamb leg and stock in a flameproof casserole dish and bring to the boil over high heat. Cover with a tight-fitting lid and transfer to the oven for 3 hours or until the meat is so tender it falls from the bone. Remove from the oven and cool in the stock for 1 hour, then take out the leg and place on a wire rack. Pick off the meat while it is still warm.

Return the dish to high heat and boil the stock for 20 minutes or until it reduces to a glaze consistency.

Melt 50 g butter in a deep frying pan over medium heat, add the shallot and cook until softened but not coloured. Add half the picked lamb meat and ½ cup (125 ml) of the glaze and mix well – if the mix is too wet add more meat; if it's too dry stir in a little more glaze. Add the parsley and season with salt and some of the lemon zest. Reserve the remaining glaze for later.

To prepare the cabbage leaves, bring a large saucepan of salted water to the boil. Have a bowl of iced water close by. Poach the cabbage leaves in the water for 1 minute, then remove and refresh in the iced water until cold. Place the leaves on a clean tea towel and pat dry. Spoon 1 tablespoon of the lamb mixture onto each leaf, then roll up tightly like a cigar, folding in the sides as you go.

Heat the olive oil in a large heavy-based frying pan over an induction set on 8 or a gas burner over high heat. Add a generous pinch of sea salt and the lamb loins and cook for 1 minute on each side or until they are nicely coloured. Turn the heat down, add the remaining butter and cook for a further 3 minutes, turning the loins twice more and basting well with the butter.

Add a squeeze of lemon and a pinch of lemon zest to the loins. Add the cabbage rolls, ½ cup (125 ml) of the remaining glaze and the thyme sprigs. Simmer for 30 seconds. Take the pan off the heat, the remove the loins and rest for 5 minutes.

To serve, carve the loins in half lengthways and either return to the pan and allow your guests to help themselves or arrange on indivual plates with the cabbage rolls and extra thyme sprigs.

Smoked eggplant puree

Serves 4

The traditional Maori method of cooking foods over hot coals in the ground covered by earth gives them a delicate smoked flavour and aroma. You'll find these characteristics in this eggplant recipe which, as it happens, is a classic accompaniment for lamb.

2 eggplants (aubergines)
100 g tahini
½ cup (150 g) mayonnaise
juice of 1 lemon
salt and pepper
pinch of ground cumin (optional)

Using a chargrill or barbecue, roast the eggplants on all sides until the skin becomes black. This will take about 20 minutes. The eggplant will lose its shape as it cooks and there will be a lot of water loss – this is fine.

When the eggplants are cooked and soft, remove them from the heat and drain in a colander. Allow to cool, then peel off the skin and remove the stalks, discarding both. Don't be tempted to wash off the blackened skin as you will lose much of the smoked flavour. Put the flesh back in the colander and press to remove any excess moisture.

Transfer the eggplant to a liquidiser or food processor and blend on full power until smooth. While continuing to blend, slowly add the tahini and mayonnaise. Season with lemon juice, salt and pepper and finish with a pinch of ground cumin, if using.

Blackcurrant jelly with Anzac crumble and sabayon

Serves 4

Did you know that New Zealand is the largest producer of blackcurrants in the world? I told you that I would learn a lot from writing this book! Normally I find blackcurrants too tart and uninteresting in their raw form but the fruit in Auckland was big, juicy and very sweet, and inspired the recipe below. A little trick I use for early-season berries is to put them in the oven for several minutes before serving. It seems to take away the tartness.

The true home of Anzac biscuits is hotly contested by the Kiwis. They won't get away with it! I simply won't allow it! But in the spirit of Miele harmony I have included the recipe here. Two things before you start: the jelly needs to set overnight, so start this recipe a day ahead, and you'll need a cooking thermometer to make the sabayon.

250 g blackcurrants

Blackcurrant jelly
400 g frozen blackcurrants, thawed
1 tablespoon caster sugar
3 × 2 g gold gelatine leaves
1 litre iced water
100 ml water

Anzac crumble
2¼ cups (200 g) rolled oats
2½ cups (200 g) desiccated coconut
1⅓ cups (200 g) plain flour
125 g brown sugar
125 g caster sugar
250 g butter
150 g manuka honey or other
   strong-flavoured honey
1 teaspoon bicarbonate of soda

Sabayon
5 egg yolks
⅓ cup (75 g) caster sugar
1 vanilla bean, split and seeds scraped

Start by making the jelly. Place the blackcurrants and sugar in a small saucepan over medium heat and stir until the sugar has dissolved. Allow to cool to room temperature, then place in food processor for 5 minutes until smooth.

Meanwhile, soak the gelatine leaves in the iced water until softened.

Combine the blackcurrant puree and 100 ml water in a small saucepan over medium heat, bring to the boil, then remove from the heat. Squeeze the excess water from the gelatine leaves and add to the puree. Whisk until they have dissolved completely, then pour into a small ceramic serving dish. Set in the fridge overnight.

Preheat the oven on intensive bake to 160°C and grease a baking tray.

The crumble is really a biscuit dough crushed to form a crumble. Place the oats, coconut, flour and sugars in a bowl and rub together using the tips of your fingers. Melt the butter and honey in a small saucepan over medium heat, add the bicarbonate of soda and whisk until fully combined. It will foam up quite dramatically, but will settle down again. Pour into the dry ingredients and mix with a wooden spoon until combined. Spread the mixture over the prepared tray to a thickness of about 1 cm and bake for 7–8 minutes or until pale golden. While the biscuit is still warm, break it up into large crumbs. Keep the oven on to warm the blackcurrants.

Just before serving, make the sabayon. Combine the egg yolks, sugar and vanilla seeds in a large metal bowl. Bring a large saucepan of water to the boil, then reduce the heat to an induction set on 5 or low heat on a gas burner. Place the bowl over the simmering water and start to whisk immediately. There is no point in whisking furiously until the egg yolks have reached 50°C (test with a cooking thermometer); when they do, whisk vigorously until the mixture reaches 70°C, at which point the mixture will start to thicken. Whisk until you can write a figure of eight that stays clearly defined for 1 second after completing.

Meanwhile, spread out the blackcurrants on a baking tray and heat in the oven for 5 minutes.

Place a large spoonful of jelly on each plate, followed by a spoonful of warmed blackcurrants, then a spoonful of Anzac crumble. Finish with the warm sabayon and serve immediately.

Visitor tips

Bars

Golden Dawn
134 Ponsonby Rd, Ponsonby
☎ +64 9376 9929
goldendawn.co.nz
From the owners of Wellington's famed Matterhorn comes this recent arrival. Take in some tunes from the rotating live acts, down a few racy cocktails, and soak it all up with a serve of juicy lamb ribs or their exceptional 'fish butty'.

Mea Culpa
3/175 Ponsonby Rd, Ponsonby
☎ +64 9376 4460
Don't let the rustic interior fool you; this intimate Ponsonby local pushes out some serious cocktails and a smart wine list with tasty treats to match.

Hotels

Cape Kidnappers
446 Clifton Road, Te Awanga, Hawke's Bay
☎ +64 6875 1900
capekidnappers.com
For me the ultimate getaway is flying into Napier for a round of golf, only to lose all 12 balls on one of the most challenging but scenic courses I have had the privilege to play on. Cape Kidnappers is the name: a luxurious rural hotel on stunning grounds where you can feel as if you are the only guests. Follow golf with an intimate dinner with your beloved by an open fire. Finish with a nightcap in the log cabin, then get up and do it all again.

Mollies
6 Tweed Street, St Mary's Bay
☎ +64 9376 3489
mollies.co.nz
With only seven bedrooms/suites this place feels more like staying in a mate's house than a hotel. A mate who is extremely loaded, with style to match, but is still thrifty enough to charge you for utilities. It has all I want: small gym, free wi-fi, great breakfast and rooms that are luxurious but not over the top.

Restaurants

The French Cafe
210 Symonds Street, Eden Terrace
☎ +64 9377 1911
thefrenchcafe.co.nz
Auckland's go-to destination for contemporary European special occasion dining. Husband and wife team Simon and Creghan Wright helm the kitchen and front-of-house respectively, reaping numerous plaudits along the way, including Supreme Winner of the 2013 Metro restaurant of the year awards. Impeccable service and a top wine list, with special fresh juices for the designated driver.

Masu
90 Federal St, Auckland
☎ +64 9363 6278
skycityauckland.co.nz/restaurants/masu
Nic Watt's contemporary Japanese restaurant and bar in Sky City's Federal Street dining precinct is all about fresh, local produce, as befits its open-grill cuisine. With a clean, sparse fit-out, lively atmosphere and menu to match, this is the place for consistent, quality Japanese with a few bold surprises thrown in.

Merediths
365 Dominion Road, Mount Eden
☎ +64 9623 3140
merediths.co.nz
Winner of the Cuisine NZ Restaurant of the Year Award and Best New Restaurant in Metro/Audi Restaurant of the Year Awards, Merediths Restaurant is owned and run by recently appointed Miele New Zealand ambassador chef, Michael Meredith. It's an intimate fine dining restaurant with seating to a maximum of forty people, and focuses on nothing other than providing remarkable food, superb wine and inviting hospitality.

Sidart →
Three Lamps Plaza, 283 Ponsonby Rd, Ponsonby
☎ +64 9360 2122
sidart.co.nz
Sid Sahrawat is Auckland's answer to Heston Blumenthal, and his unassuming restaurant tucked away in Ponsonby is punching above its weight. Go for innovative, experimental dishes and magnificent views of the Auckland skyline. The daring should submit to the experimental Test Kitchen on Tuesdays where $80 will buy you eight set courses (optional, matched with wines for another $80), while Chef's Table on Wednesdays admits diners to the kitchen's inner sanctum for some culinary pampering.

Berlin

This city is constantly evolving,
with centuries of cultural heritage
providing a backdrop for the new and edgy.

This city has proffered an unconditional apology to the world for the sins of its fathers. Its past has moulded its present. Where else in the world exists such a culture, its functionality equalled only by its edginess? I can't think of anywhere else that I can recommend to every age group and every demographic, regardless of gender, race or religion as I can this city. Berlin is guaranteed to excite and educate.

Berlin is Miele's home city, so I have an opportunity to spend some time with the company's proprietors, Dr Markus Miele and Dr Reinhard Zinkann. Both are true gentlemen and never speak German in front of me. Markus captains the ship and Reinhard sails it. If I want to know about classical art or the history of a city, I ask Reinhard. If I want to know about modern art, politics or tax policy, I ask Markus. I feel incredibly privileged to call these men my friends. The Miele hierarchy encourages this sort of communication. In a normal working week both men can be seen eating at the staff canteen in the Gütesloh head office. Dr Miele and Dr Zinkann encourage their team members to talk about their company openly and frequently, with pride and humour.

I am less than a week into the second stint of the European trips but I'm flagging. The dinners are being met with great feedback. The German Miele kitchen team are very organised and a pleasure to work with, giving me a 'mental break' of sorts. The extra day in Berlin gives me a chance to come up for air a little and visit a few of the city's museums and art galleries.

Taxis in Berlin deserve a special mention. They might not be not the cleanest or newest cars on the road but they might be the coolest. My taxi has travelled over 630 000 kilometres and first hit the road in 1989. I do a deal for half a day, at a fixed rate of 250€ for five hours. My driver's name is Klaus. Before the integration of Europe, Klaus would earn the equivalent of 25€ per hour. Now he is lucky to earn 5€. Therefore, taxis now have to make ends meet in other ways, and what better tour guide can you have than a taxi driver with thirty years on the road in Berlin? A good concierge will have someone like Klaus in their black book.

And if you have time, a good start to exploring the city is the free guided walking tours, which offer a real insight into the city. They take around four hours but they are well worth the time. They can be booked through the concierge in your hotel. Also keep an eye out for new apps available on your phone; these are constantly evolving and are particularly good if you want to explore the city's art. ●

1–2   Standert bike shop and cafe, which sells bikes and does repairs as well as serving food and coffee. Just the thing to replenish body and soul after a bike ride.

3   Pretzel sellers abound on street corners.

4–5   There is art everywhere you look in this city, from colourful tiles on lovely old buildings to the most extraordinary graffiti.

6   The new dome of the Reichstag, built to
    symbolise the reunification of Germany.
7   The Field of Stelae in the Holocaust Memorial.
8   The Brandenburg Gate, familiar from movies
    and Nazi propaganda.
9   In Le Petit Felix at the Hotel Adlon Kemplinski,
    where I prepared canapes for a group of
    Australian electrical retailers and suppliers,
    in town to visit IFA, Europe's most prestigious
    trade show for electronics, while they enjoyed
    pre-dinner drinks.
10 The dome of the French Cathedral, from which
    visitors can enjoy a panoramic view of Berlin.

Falafels

Serves 4

Berliners are adamant that if the doner kebab wasn't invented in Berlin by Turkish immigrants then it was certainly perfected by them. Over the past decade most bratwurst stands have been replaced by kebab shops and I was initially a bit surprised at how popular their vegetarian counterpart, falafels, are. But then again, I never go to the trouble of cooking these very simple patties at home, so why not?

2 brown onions, finely chopped
4 cloves garlic, crushed
2 tablespoons freshly ground coriander seeds
1 tablespoon freshly ground cumin seeds
2 × 400 g cans chickpeas, drained and rinsed
2 bunches flat-leaf parsley, leaves picked,
    washed and roughly chopped
2 eggs, beaten
sea salt
1 cup (250 ml) extra virgin olive oil
3⅓ cups (500 g) plain flour
8 pieces flatbread, cut into wedges

Garlic mayonnaise
2 heads garlic
500 g good-quality Japanese mayonnaise

Tabouli
100 g cooked bulgur
1 pickled cucumber, roughly chopped
good handful of mint, roughly chopped
good handful of flat-leaf parsley,
    roughly chopped
1 clove garlic, finely chopped
finely grated zest and juice of 1 lemon
1 brown onion, finely chopped
2 tomatoes, finely chopped
100 ml olive oil
sea salt

Place the onion, garlic, coriander, cumin, chickpeas and parsley in a food processor and pulse to form a nice crumble. Tip the mixture into a large bowl. Slowly add the beaten egg and lightly mix it in. Check for seasoning, then add 1 tablespoon olive oil and sprinkle in the flour, mixing until it just comes together. Transfer to the refrigerator for 30 minutes.

Meanwhile, to make the garlic mayo, preheat the oven on the conventional setting to 160°C. Place the whole heads of garlic on a baking tray and roast for 10–15 minutes or until the garlic is soft and slightly caramelised. Remove from the oven and, while still a little warm, squeeze the garlic cloves out of their skins and mix with the mayonnaise to form a smooth paste.

Reduce the oven temperature to 150°C.

To make the tabouli, combine all the ingredients (except the salt) in a bowl. Taste, and season with salt. Store in the fridge until ready to serve.

Heat a little olive oil in a frying pan over medium–high heat and fry a small piece of the falafel mixture to check the consistency. It should hold together – if it is too wet, add a touch more flour to it; if it's too dry, add a little more olive oil, then put it back in the fridge for 30 minutes.

Shape the falafel mixture into little 3–4 cm patties. You can freeze some for later if you don't want to cook them all now.

Heat a large frying pan over medium–high heat and drizzle in the remaining olive oil. Add the falafels and fry for 2 minutes or until nice and golden, then turn them over and repeat on the other side. Transfer the falafels to a non-stick baking tray and place in the oven for 5 minutes until heated through. At the same time, put the flatbread in the oven for 5 minutes to warm up.

Serve the falafels with the tabouli, garlic mayonnaise and flatbread on the side.

Ham with pease pudding and mustard potatoes

Serves 4

Having seen how many food stalls on the streets of Berlin serve this dish of mashed legumes and root vegetables I cannot understand why the British insist the dish is theirs. I really enjoyed eating it sandwiched inside a type of pocket bread. To get the most out of it, ask your butcher for the freshest possible pork knuckles, but apart from that feel free to add your own take by exchanging vegetables and herbs for others that may suit the seasons.

2 pork knuckles
1 head garlic, broken into cloves
sea salt
5 bay leaves
10 juniper berries
10 black peppercorns
5 sprigs marjoram
good handful of flat-leaf parsley,
    sprigs and all
2 litres chicken stock

Mustard potatoes
1 kg new potatoes, well washed
sea salt
handful of flat-leaf parsley sprigs (optional)
100 g dijon mustard
20 g honey
½ handful dill, finely chopped

Pease pudding
2½ cups (500 g) yellow split peas, soaked
    in cold water overnight
2 tablespoons grapeseed oil
1 brown onion, finely chopped
1 carrot, finely chopped
2 tablespoons malt vinegar
2 bay leaves
50 g butter, cut into chunks
sea salt and freshly ground white pepper

Rinse the pork knuckles in cold water and place them in a large saucepan. Add the garlic, salt, bay leaves, juniper berries, peppercorns, marjoram and parsley, then cover with the chicken stock. Bring to the boil, then reduce the heat to low and simmer gently for 3 hours or until the meat is tender and falling off the bone. Remove the pan from the heat and allow the pork to cool in the stock.

To make the mustard potatoes, place the potatoes in a wide-based saucepan and pour in just enough water to cover. Season the water well (potatoes can absorb so much flavour so don't be shy with the seasoning), and add the parsley sprigs, if using. Bring to the boil, then reduce the heat and simmer until the potatoes are just tender but still have a slight crunch to them. Take the pan off the heat and allow the potatoes to cool completely in the water, then drain well. Mix together the mustard, honey and dill and stir through the potatoes.

For the pease pudding, drain the split peas, then place in a large saucepan, cover with water and cook until tender – about 40 minutes. Drain. Heat the grapeseed oil in a large saucepan, add the onion and carrot and cook gently over low heat until softened but not coloured. Add the spilt peas, vinegar and bay leaves, then take the pan off the heat and stir in the butter until melted and combined. Season to taste.

Shred the pork into bite-sized pieces and combine with the pease pudding. Moisten with some of the pork cooking liquid and serve with the mustard potatoes.

Marzipan cake with rumtopf fruits

Serves 4

In a way, it's better if you buy the rumtopf (literally, rum pot) because the traditional version can be time consuming to make yourself, but for adventurous cooks or those who have their own fruit trees, go ahead! The idea for this recipe came about when I was walking through the centre of Berlin – I was amazed at how ornate the rumtopf jars can be, and how many varieties there are. This would make a great Christmas Day delight.

melted butter, for brushing
250 g butter
250 g caster sugar
250 g marzipan, roughly chopped
4 large eggs (you need 250 g in total)
⅓ cup (50 g) plain flour
finely grated zest of 1 lemon
8 strawberries, hulled and cut in half
⅔ cup (100 g) blueberries
20 raspberries
mint sprigs, to garnish
vanilla ice-cream, to serve

Rumtopf
6 apples, peeled, cored and cut into quarters
4 pears, peeled, cored and cut into quarters
4 plums, cut into wedges, stones removed
20 green seedless grapes
3 cups (660 g) brown sugar
3 cups (750 ml) overproof rum (54%)

Rumtopf is a dish that needs to be prepared over time. You essentially start with the harder fruits and gradually add the softer fruits, checking the mixture weekly. The general ratio is for every 2 parts of fruit you need 1 part sugar and approximately 3 cups (750 ml) rum. Spoon the fruit into the rumtopf jar and fill with enough rum to cover the fruit. After the last fruit is added, leave for 6 weeks, topping up with rum if needed.

Preheat the oven on intensive bake to 160°C. Line a baking tray with baking paper and brush with melted butter.

Using an electric mixer fitted with the whisk attachment, cream the butter and sugar until pale, then gradually beat in the marzipan. Add the eggs and beat until very smooth, then sift in the flour and add the lemon zest. Pour the batter into the baking tray and bake for 30 minutes or until a skewer inserted into the centre comes out clean. Remove from the oven and leave to cool completely in the tin at room temperature.

To serve, use a round cutter to cut out 4 portions of cake. Spoon over the rum liquid from the rumtopf and leave to soak for 20 minutes. Spoon the fruit over and around the cake, garnish with the fresh berries and mint sprigs, and serve with vanilla ice-cream.

Visitor tips

Bars and pubs

The Bar at the Grand
Hirtenstrasse 4, 10178
☎ +49 30 2789 099 555
the-grand-berlin.com/en/bar
This is without doubt the hottest bar in
Berlin at the moment. A huge outdoor
courtyard serves good, simple food such
as grilled steaks and pastas. The quaint,
historic decor of the ground floor houses
a very professional bar team churning out
all sorts of cocktails, specialising in sours.

Prater Beer Garden
Kastanienallee 7–9, 10435
☎ +49 30 448 56 88
pratergarten.de
The huge expanse of long tables and
bench seating oozes atmosphere, while
a wood-fired oven pumps out thin, crispy
pizzas. Several beers are on tap and you
can enjoy a cold one amongst the fairy
lights draped over 100-year-old chestnut
trees. The menu includes such classics as
Königsberger Klopse (meatballs in caper
sauce), wiener schnitzel and *Senfeier
mit Quetschkartoffeln* (mustard eggs and
mash). The day I visit, their famous wild
goose is on the menu; it's a little dry but
has incredible flavour, served with wild
mushrooms and a light cucumber and dill
salad. This dish alone is worth the journey.

Soho House Club Bar
Torstrasse 1, 10119
☎ +49 30 40 50 44
sohohouseberlin.com
Try your luck at smooth-talking the
reception team, or put your name on
the guest list in advance. The bar is alive
with the young generation of Berliners
socialising and networking. The air is thick
with the smell of success. Cocktails are the
order of the day, and on a fine summer's
night, venture up to the pool bar and look
out over East Berlin.

Gardens

Prinzessinnengarten
(Princess Garden) ↓
Prinzenstrasse 35–38/
Prinzesinnenstrasse 15
(U8 Moritzplatz)
☎ +49 176 24 33 22 97
prinzessinnengarten.net/about
To my amazement, behind some rusted old
fences and piles of rubble I find an oasis
of 400–500 species of plants, including
thirty-five different types of tomatoes,
and a seed bank, bordered by old shipping
containers converted to toilets, kitchens
and a bar. Claudia and Matthieus, two
of the custodians, show me through the
garden, which sits atop the rubble of an
industrial warehouse which was bombed
to oblivion during the Second World War.
'We want to make a difference to local
Berliners,' Matthias says. It is run by
volunteers who receive very cheap prices
in return, but the public is welcome to buy
herbs as well as soil for balcony gardens.
Everything has flavour and is organic. They
are open for lunch and dinner seven days,
dinner being garden pizzas and locally
brewed beer. The setting is truly amazing.

Cafes

Cafe Einstein
Kurfürstenstrasse 58, 10785
☎ +49 30 263 91 90
cafeeinstein.com/en
Very traditional and has been there
for years. It's within metres of the
Miele Center.

Hotels

Hotel Das Stue
Drakestrasse 1, 10787
☎ +49 30 31 17 22
das-stue.com
Patricia Urquiola's furniture designs are
some of the most sought after in the world,
designed to be both special occasion and
everyday luxury in the one piece. When
I read that Patricia had put her hand to
interior designing a hotel, I was intrigued.
Located in the old Danish Embassy and
backing on to the Berlin Zoo, the location
is peerless. The well-appointed, luxurious
rooms are small but ask for one with a
balcony. Staff are excellent, the concierges
willing to go out of their way to help. The
ground floor bar serves some excellent
cocktails, both inside with a small cinema
playing black-and-white films, or outside
in the expansive courtyard, where you can
gaze at roaming emus in the Berlin Zoo.

Soho House ←
Torstrasse 1, 10119
☎ +49 30 40 50 44
sohohouseberlin.com
I *love* my showers. After a long day at
work or a tough work-out, my shower is
my reward. I have now discovered the
only hotel in the world that has a better
shower than mine. No fancy buttons, just
an enormous, old-fashioned rainwater
showerhead inset from the ceiling, along
with a large stone seat. But wait! There is

more! With the press of a button the whole shower room turns into a *hammam*-style steam room.

My spacious room, complete with Art Deco flourishes, is very impressive. It's all about the little touches, like the beautiful tray with teas and fresh ground coffee, sugars and French press accompanied by a silver tin full of freshly baked biscuits.

The edgy decor throughout the public areas capture Berlin perfectly. Contemporary art adorns the lobby, while the lifts are lined in patched brown leather with graffiti scratched into it. The gym is the most spacious and well equipped of any boutique hotel I know.

Museums and art galleries

Boros Bunkers
Reinhardtstrasse 20, 10117
☎ **+49 30 27 59 40 65**
sammlung-boros.de
Built in 1942 as a bomb shelter during the Allied raids, this place housed well over 6000 people at the height of the war. I was surprised to find such a grandiose structure, protruding five storeys out of the ground. Once inside you understand why it's still standing. There are eighty cell-like rooms and it once operated as an illegal brothel and sex club; it was swiftly closed by local authorities before being converted to an incredible collection of modern artworks, including some by renowned photographer Wolfgang Tillmans. Christian Boros purchased the building in 2003, remodelling it and placing a penthouse apartment at the top. Open on weekends only and you need to book a guided tour, which is easily done.

The Hoffman Collection
Sophienstrasse 21, 10178
☎ **+49 30 28 49 91 20**
sammlung-hoffmann.de
Erika Hoffman opens up her expansive apartment, by appointment only, each Saturday to small groups. Erika and her late husband, Rolf, started collecting works in 1968. A curated guided tour takes about ninety minutes and includes works from Antony Gormley. Guided tours can be booked quite simply over the phone.

Käthe Kollwitz Museum
Fasanenstr 25, 10719
☎ **+49 30 882 52 10**
kaethe-kollwitz.de/museum-en.htm
Dedicated to the work of the extraordinary artist Kathe Kollwitz, renowned for her self-portraits and commitment to difficult subjects such as poverty, war and death as well as happier themes.

Museum Island
Spree Island, Spree River, Mitte
visitberlin.de/en/spot/museum-island
Five museums on an island in the Spree river. The buildings housing them are awe-inspiring. Beware, there are a lot of tourists, but space abounds, with generous gardens enclosing the spectacular buildings. Leave a whole day to explore. The Old National Gallery has works up to the Impressionist era.

Restaurants

Alpenstueck Restaurant and Cafe →
Gartenstrasse 9, 10115
☎ **+49 30 217 516 46**
alpenstueck.com
This truly Germanic bistro and cafe is situated amongst the fashionable back streets in the heart of the Mitte, which means centre. This Bavarian eatery is split in two. Daytime cafe to the right, night-time bistro across the road on the left. Try the fried veal dumplings with spinach and burnt butter. A good little local and a nice spot for the traveller looking to escape the usual tourist traps.

The Bird
Prenzlauer Berg, Am Falkplatz 5
☎ **+49 30 51 05 32 83**
thebirdinberlin.com
They all say this local rock 'n' roll hangout has the best burger in town. *Da Bird Burger* is two medium-sized patties grilled over charcoal, served medium-rare and smothered in melted cheese, large pickles and grilled bacon, then sandwiched in a flat, soft bread roll. The plate is loaded with chips and salad, all for 12 €. The vegetarian burger is delicious, made up of chopped grilled field mushrooms and crushed potato with some finely mashed pulses, then moulded into patties and pan fried.

Curry 36
Various branches – see website for details.
curry36.de
Curry 36 is a small chain of sausage shops. Named after the postal code of the area of Kreuzberg, this is home to the famous sausage curry-wurst: the true native Berlin street food. Round the clock, dozens of people line up to grab their paper plate of grilled, sliced sausage smothered in a rich tomato sauce and sprinkled with curry powder. Surprisingly, the sausage itself is very delicate and smooth, the curry powder subtle. I try two types, the skinless *o. darm*, and *mit der darm* curry, which is with skin. Both are delicious, with chips smothered in mayonnaise, ketchup and chilli salt. The *Deliktasse-weiner*, which is a boiled sausage, looks great, especially with potato salad drowned in mayonnaise. I am amazed to be told that young people are not keen on this sort of food, so these shops are now becoming scarce, replaced by kebab shops.

The prices are ridiculously cheap: 1€ (40 cents) per sausage! Be part of Berlin and stop for a wurst.

Katerschmaus →
Michaelkirchstrasse 23, 10179
☎ +49 30 51 05 21 34
katerholzig.de
Located in a disused industrial textiles
factory in East Berlin, this place feels as if
a bunch of extras from the first *Mad Max*
film got lost and decided to set up camp. No
such luck; everyone wants to join the fun!
There's a restaurant on the third-floor roof,
four bars, three nightclubs and a market,
all set on the canal. I have never seen such
resourceful up-cycling and recycling in my
life: old doors are now bar tops and disused
tyres are now flooring. The food is hugely
popular, and people are happy to queue for
an hour for it. The pizzas served at the bar
by the canal are sensational.

Kimchi Princess
Skalitzer Strasse 36/Manteuffelstr 10999
☎ +49 16 34 58 02 03
kimchiprincess.com
This is the latest hip place in Berlin. Korean
food is currently a worldwide phenomenon
and Berlin is not immune.

Maroush
Adalbertstrasse 93, 10999
☎ +49 30 69 53 61 71
maroush-berlin.de
We didn't actually visit this Lebanese place,
but it's very popular. Berlin is very good on
Middle Eastern food generally.

Restaurant Cinco by Paco Perez
Drakestrasse 1; Das Stue Hotel Berlin
Tiergarten, 10787
☎ +49 30 31 17 22
5-cinco.com

The chef here is young, but seems to have a good head on his shoulders. Food ranges from good to excellent, mainly influenced by the chef's Spanish heritage. My favourite dish? Fresh anchovies, lightly salted, drowned in olive oil then laid out on a large white plate garnished with dots of tomato sauce and what I think was anchovy puree, parsley and diced pear, backed up with some grilled flat bread rubbed generously with fresh tomato and garlic. The whole dish looked like a fancy pizza and tasted even better than it looked. There are also some great references to Germanic culture such as the chef's take on Black Forest cake. Bits of chocolate sponge nestle amongst feather-light chocolate mousse, whipped cream and cherry sorbet. The place for a glamorous, romantic night out.

Restaurant Vau ←
Mitte, Jägerstrasse 54/55
☎ +49 30 20 29 73 0
vau-berlin.de

Kolja Kleeberg has owned and run this Michelin-starred restaurant for eighteen years. The dining room has a spectacular curved brass ceiling and glorious artwork depicting his home town, Cologne. Dishes range from avant garde to classic Berlin, my favourite being the black pudding sausage cooked with a lentil stew and served simply with warm, dense rye bread. During the summer the outdoor courtyard is a great lunch spot. The food is good, the service excellent and the wine list fantastic, featuring many German varietals and styles not found outside Germany.

Brussels

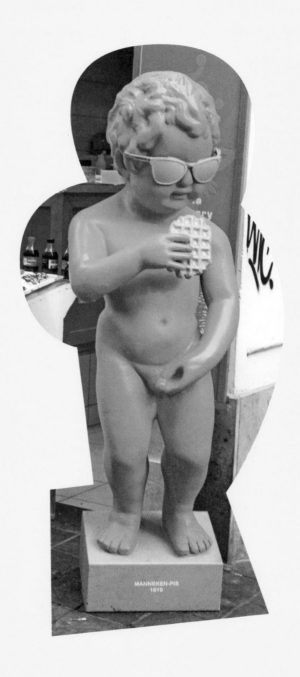

We eat mussels, waffles and eel,
----
and encounter a rather unusual
----
statue everywhere.

Sunday in this city is tough. As we find out the hard way, most of the top restaurants close on Sundays and Mondays. What do I know about the food culture of Brussels? There are mussels, both steamed and raw, french fries, chocolate, *tin tin* (pronounced 'tan tan') beer, and of course waffles. It's also famous for linen, lace and tapestry, but I'm sure there's more to it and in my forty-eight hours here I'm determined to find it.

Your first stop should be the jaw-droppingly beautiful and unique Grand Place. It's a bit of a tourist trap but great food and drink can still be found just off the main square. Eel with sorrel sauce is a must – eel is one of the city's favourite dishes.

Love of country is evident everywhere you look, and it is heartening to be among a people so proud of who they are and where they come from. This city has proper seasons, so food changes and evolves through the year. Most ignorant muppets, myself included, would nominate the cliched dish of mussels and chips as the *Belge* national meal, but in fact these are rarely served together and mussels are actually not served all year round. The season is quite short, from the first of August until the end of October. In those months, mussels are in abundance and should be ordered whenever the opportunity presents itself.

At home, *Stoemp*, crushed potato with vegetables, served with sausages, is a favoured dish, a very popular recipe passed down from generation to generation and made in the home kitchen. Now the Miele pressure steamer can be used to make this dish in less than ten minutes.

With a population of 1 million, I think this town is punching well above its weight. There is a formidable culture here, a powerful sense of connectedness between people and place. ●

1–2   Pedestrian-only streets, cobblestones and outdoor cafes make Brussels a city where you can take life at a relaxed pace.

3   The former stock exchange building (the Bourse) is now used as an exhibition hall.

4   Guild worker statues, representing medieval guilds, in the Place du Petit Sablon.

5   The Cathedral of Our Lady.

6   La Cure Gourmande, a treasure trove of sweets, biscuits and chocolates.

7   Cafe Leffe, home of Leffe beer.

8   The most famous statue in Brussels, *Mannekin Pis* – 'Little Man Pee'. He is reproduced all over the city.

9   The Place du Petit Sablon.

10   Mussels are the city's most recognisable dish.

11   With the owners of Comme Chez Soi, Laurence and Lionel Rigolet.

12–13 Iconic local *friterie*, Maison Antoine.

14   Seafood restaurant Les Crustaces.

15   The Atomium, built to replicate the structure of an iron atom. Visitors can walk around inside the sculpture.

Eel with wild herbs

Serves 4

I admit this doesn't sound like the sort of dish I'd usually enjoy, but you must trust me on this. Eel is a national ingredient here and the Belgians certainly know how to do it justice. If eel is not available, use John Dory or slimy mackerel instead. My version is much simpler than the traditional recipe, using the butter from the pan as a simple sauce and keeping the herbs fresh rather than blended. If you manage to find an extra 10 minutes in the kitchen, juice 2 good bunches of sorrel and drizzle a spoonful over each plate before serving.

2 tablespoons grapeseed oil
2 fresh eel, each cut into 4 pieces
    (or use hot-smoked eel if unavailable)
¼ cup (35 g) plain flour
120 g butter
2 slices brown bread, crusts removed,
    cut into 2 cm pieces
juice of ½ lemon
salt flakes and freshly ground black pepper
16 baby sorrel leaves
a few sprigs flat-leaf parsley
4 sprigs chervil
8 mint leaves
8 pea shoots
8 chives, cut into 3 cm lengths
borrage or chive flowers, to garnish

Heat the grapeseed oil in a large heavy frying pan over an induction set on 7 or medium heat on a gas burner. If you are using fresh eel, coat it in flour, shaking off any excess. Add the eel to the pan and fry for 2 minutes each side. Use a skewer to test whether it is cooked – if it goes through without any resistance it's ready. Remove the eel from the pan and rest in a warm spot in the kitchen.

Deglaze the pan with 100 g butter and set aside. This is essentially the sauce.

Melt the remaining butter in a frying pan over medium–high heat and fry the bread until crisp. Remove and drain on paper towel.

Divide the eel among individual plates. Squeeze the lemon into the butter sauce and season with salt and pepper. Drizzle the sauce around each plate, and add 3–4 bread crisps per person. Scatter over the herbs and serve.

Flemish cod

Serves 4

This is a traditional dish of the simplest proportions: the freshest cod fillets you can find poached in white wine, lemon and butter, garnished with herbs and red onion rings. For an extra dimension try adding 20 well-washed mussels in the shell for the last 2 minutes of cooking time.

4 × 180 g cod fillets, skin and bones removed
200 g cultured butter, cut into 2 cm cubes
1 large red onion, cut into 1 cm thick slices
2 cups (500 ml) white wine
2 lemons
sea salt
8 sprigs flat-leaf parsley, leaves picked
8 oyster leaves or baby spinach leaves

Preheat the oven on the conventional setting to 180°C. Remove the cod fillets from the fridge and bring to room temperature.

Heat a large cast-iron flameproof casserole dish over an induction set on 8 or a gas burner over medium–high heat. Add 3 cubes of butter, then gently fry the onion rings with the flat sides down until they gain a little colour, about 5 minutes. Add the white wine and boil until it has reduced by half. Remove the onion and set aside.

Whisk the remaining butter into the wine in 3 batches, then bring to the boil. Remove the dish from the heat and add the cod, making sure it is completely covered with the butter sauce. Cover and place in the oven for about 8 minutes or until just cooked.

While the fish is cooking, remove the zest from the lemons and cut it into thin strips. Squeeze the juice from the lemons.

Test whether the fish is cooked by inserting a skewer – it should go through without any resistance. Remove the fish to a plate and let it rest. Season the sauce with lemon juice and salt, then buzz with a stick blender to create a foam.

Place the poached cod on individual plates and garnish with the onion rings, lemon zest and herbs. Sauce the fish with the butter foam at the table to impress your guests even more!

Belgian waffles

Serves 4 hungry people

I always thought that waffles were basically pancake batter cooked in a waffle iron, but this is not the case at all. These are the best waffles I have ever tasted – light and fluffy on the inside, and crisp and smoky on the outside, with just a hint of vanilla. Thank God I don't live in Belgium or I would be at least 20 kilograms heavier! The batter needs to rest for 12 hours so start this recipe a day ahead.

1 vanilla bean, split and seeds scraped
⅓ cup (80 ml) lukewarm milk
3 small eggs, separated
16 g fresh yeast (you could use 5 g dried
    yeast instead, but the result will be
    a bit different)
1⅔ cups (250 g) plain flour
1 cup (250 ml) water
200 g butter, melted and cooled
    to room temperature
dash of sparkling water
2 tablespoons melted butter, extra
4 handfuls of fresh berries, cut into 1 cm pieces
100 g caster sugar
icing sugar, for dusting
whipped cream, to serve
mint sprigs, to garnish

Add the vanilla bean and seeds to the lukewarm milk and allow to infuse for a few minutes. Strain, discarding the vanilla bean.

Whip the egg whites until soft peaks form. Set aside.

Place the yeast and lukewarm milk in a small bowl and stir to dissolve. Sift the flour into a bowl and add the egg yolks, whisking constantly. Whisk in the milk and yeast mixture, then add the water in 3 batches (you may not need it all – just enough to reach a batter consistency). Blend in the melted butter, then gently fold in the whipped egg whites. Cover and leave in the refrigerator overnight to rise.

Just before you're ready to cook the waffles add a dash of sparkling water to the batter – the consistency needs to be similar to a thick pouring cream.

Preheat the waffle iron and brush with a little of the extra melted butter.

Spoon ½ cup (125 ml) of the batter into the waffle iron – do not close it completely as the mixture will rise. Cook until nice and golden, then flip it over and cook on the other side until golden. Repeat with the remaining batter – the exact number of waffles will depend on the size of your waffle iron.

While the waffles are cooking, heat a frying pan over an induction set on 5 or a gas burner over medium heat, add the berries and sprinkle with the caster sugar. Cook for 3 minutes or until the sugar has dissolved and the mixture has reached a jam-like consistency.

Dust the waffles with icing sugar and serve with a spoonful each of whipped cream and berry jam. Garnish with mint sprigs.

Visitor tips

Bars and cafes

Brussels is not really a bar city. Every cafe serves beer and wine and this is where most drinks are consumed. Young people, however, do enjoy dedicated bars where the local gin, genever, is making a resurgence.

L'Archiduc
Antoine Dansaertstraat 6, 1000
☎ +32 2 512 06 52
archiduc.net/en
One of the oldest bars, if not *the* oldest in Brussels. Central location and late opening hours make this bar a must for a modern cocktail or a local genever aged in oak.

Cafe Belga
Flagey Plein 18, 1050
☎ +32 2 640 35 08
cafebelga.be
This cafe looks over the Place Flagey, a reformed square once noted as 'no-go' area of Brussels but now an up-and-coming inner-city apartment area. A former radio and television station above made this joint famous, and they still conduct outdoor performances from time to time. Note that cafes in Belgium are generally not known for coffee; they are where you get a beer!

L'Entree des Artistes et Aperol
42 Place du Grand Sablon, 1000
☎ +32 2 502 31 61
lentreedesartistex.be
A quaint little bar off the Petit Sablon. Sit outside, soak up the refined atmosphere and order off the weekly changing blackboard.

Le Marche St Gery
Place Saint-Géry 1, 1000
☎ +32 2 502 44 24
hallessaintgery.be
Set in an old church hall dating back to 1802, this glorious monument to Brussels past plays tourist information centre by day and beer hall with a small menu available by night. The neighbourhood is dotted with plenty of bars and pubs, all boasting a fabulous atmosphere well into the night.

The Monk ↓
Rue Sainte-Catherine 42, 1000
☎ +32 2 503 08 80
monk.be
Lively bar that serves simple snacks in a nice part of the city. They are famous for their cured hams and sausages.

Bistros

Bistro Henri
Rue de Flandre 113, 1000
☎ +32 2 218 00 08
restohenri.be
Great quirky bistro serving classic dishes with a modern sensibility.

Bistro la Marie Joseph →
Brandhoutkaai 47, 1000
☎ +32 2 218 05 96
lamariejoseph.be
The fourth-generation owner of this establishment, Sarah Niels, strolls up to our table to welcome us. The space has a light modern feel with a lovely terrace overlooking the square. Bustling and at

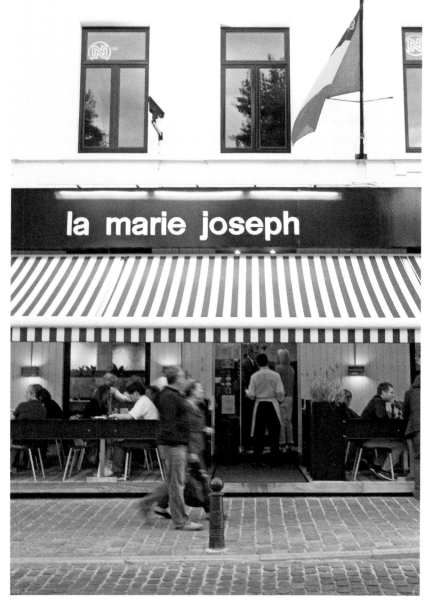

times frantic, the bistro still retains a sense of intimacy. We are in search of the famous *Paling in 't groen,* eel in hot green sauce. While we wait, Sarah brings out another classic, *Caricoles* – baby sea snails in their shells, simmered in a court-bouillon of vegetables, herbs and most importantly, hot piemonte peppers. Served cold in the shell, the flavour is incredibly intense with a great peppery end note. Next is baby shrimp in a house-made *croquette aux crevettes grises d'Oostende.*

The eel finally arrives and, my god, it is worth the wait. A thick green sauce with more texture and acid than I expected. Sarah tells me the secret of the sauce: it contains seven herbs: watercress, parsley, spinach, lemongrass, sage, sorrel and chervil, all blended into the hot stock just before serving.

Bistro Selecto
Rue De Flandre 95–97, 1000
☎ **+32 2 511 40 95**
leselecto.com
The bistro that has the 'it' factor at the moment; go there to see and be seen.

Bistro au Vieux Saint Martin
Grand Sablon 38, 1000
☎ **+32 2 512 64 76**
auvieuxsaintmartin.be
From the same family who owned brasserie Marie Saint-Joseph comes this charming little bistro. Very ornate and it is full of locals who use this space for their ever-changing daily needs: coffee, tartines, lunch or a more substantial dinner and dessert. There are not many inner-city neighbourhood bistros that could compete with this one's setting and atmosphere.

La Brasserie de Bruxelles ↓
Place Old Corn Exchange 39, 1000
Brussels Centre
☎ +32 2 513 98 12
labrasseriedebruxelles.be
Brasserie de Bruxelles is, in local terms,
a new bistro – only opened *five* years ago!
The menu is expansive with all the classics,
and it is good. Atmosphere is busy and
noisy. Desserts are a highlight: the simple
combination of vanilla ice cream, whipped
cream and warm chocolate sauce has the
texture of silk. The waffle is thick, yet light
as a feather with even lighter whipped
cream Chantilly. The hint of smoke in the
crisp pastry is a wonder.

Chocolate, pastry and bread

Neuhaus Chocolates
Naamsestraat 103
☎ +32 2 514 19 65
neuhauschocolates.com
This world-famous store sells its limited-
edition ranges instore as well as many
boxed gifts. The shop was originally a
pharmacy and its founder, Jean Neuhaus,
had the genius idea of coating his
medicines in chocolate to make them
more palatable. The rest is history.

Le Pain Quotidien ↓
Rue des Sablons 11, 1000
☎ +32 2 513 51 54
lepainquotidien.be
This is the place to go for bread. Alain
Coumont started the original bakery in
1990, as a teenager, baking organic *miche*
bread out of his garage. Today there are
185 shops in nineteen countries. One thing
I like is that Alain has a zero marketing
budget. He relies 100 per cent on store
performance; customers spread the word.
'The customer needs to buy my bread for
the right reasons,' he says. Breakfast here
is simple and cheap. Try the homemade
lemonades and coolers.

Lola Bistro
Place du Grand Sablon 33, 1000
☎ +32 2 514 24 60
restolola.be
A more modern take on the classic
bistro, next to the Poltona Frau shop.
Classic bistro dishes are given a light,
contemporary touch. In asparagus
season they have an 'asparagus festival'.

Pierre Marcolini Chocolates ↓
Rue des Minimes 1, 1000
☎ +32 2 514 12 06
marcolini.be/#/en
First and foremost, Pierre Marcolini
is a pastry chef, one who developed a
passion for chocolate. In 1995 he turned
his hand to chocolate and opened his
'boutique' on Sablon. That initial shop
front has now expanded to twenty stores
worldwide. Marcolini is famous for his
relentless search for the white cocoa bean,
'porcelana', which gives his chocolate an
incredible silkiness and perfect melting
temperature. He naturally ferments all
his beans. He also tells me that all his
chocolates are a minimum of 72 per cent
cocoa mass. Every six months, the shop
is reinvented to reflect fashion and the
seasons. When I visit, the concept is the
secret garden; all pralines, pastries and
jellies are based on the herbs and spices
found in the gardens of Belgium. My
favourite is pineapple sage ganache in
a thin, crisp bitter chocolate shell topped
with yellow chocolate.

Les Tartes de Françoise ↓
Avenue de l'Hippodrome, 75, 1050 Ixelles
☎ +32 2 640 88 41
tartes.be
A true 'Atelier' house. A small, very discreet
door leads to a narrow hallway and large
kitchen at the end, where a small array of
tarts and flans are on display with the chefs
filling boxes by the dozen. There are over
a dozen of these stores in Belgium. The
baked tomato and mushroom flan is their
specialty, in my opinion.

Wittamer Patissiere
Place du Grand Sablon, 1000
☎ +32 2 512 37 42
wittamer.com/en
This is where the now-retired king buys his
pastries, believe it or not. The store boasts
some great picnic basket fillers: salads and
filled baguettes, little cakes and ice creams.
The place to order your wedding cake.

Coffee

Coffee Or ↓
Auguste Orts 9 I, 1000
☎ +32 2 511 74 00
orcoffee.be
Located very centrally, Coffee Or serves
brewed, *chemex*, French press and espresso
single-origin coffees to local aficionados in
a bolthole of a shop that is very busy. You
may have to wait for a seat. Alternatively,
get takeaway brewed coffee from Rwanda
and go for a wander through the Grand
Place. Food is limited but the chocolate
brownies are of course Belgian in origin so
they don't disappoint. All beans are roasted
on site. Free wi-fi.

Hotels

Restaurants

Hotel Amigo
Rue de l'Amigo 1, 1000
☎ +32 2 547 47 47
roccofortehotels.com/hotels-and-resorts/hotel-amigo/
Just off the Grand Place, surrounded by historic laneways, this place oozes atmosphere. Well priced but not cheap. Standard rooms are a nice size. Free wi-fi. The Italian restaurant, Bocconi, is highly recommended if you get sick of mussels!

Pillows Hotel
Place Rouppe 17, 1000
☎ +32 2 204 00 40
sandton.eu/en/brusselspillows
A great little designer hotel opposite Belgium's finest restaurant, Comme Chez Soi. A little out of the way from bustling tourist spots, the recent renovation has converted the once-tired decor into that of a tasteful and opulent boutique hotel.

Steigenberger Hotel
Avenue Louise 71, 1050
☎ +32 2 542 42 42
en.steigenberger.com/Brussels/Steigenberger-Grandhotel
The most famous grand hotel in Brussels. It is here that presidents, prime ministers and Justin Beiber stay when in town. Try the bar upstairs for a special occasion but make sure to be well dressed.

Comme Chez Soi ↓
Place Rouppe 23, 1000
☎ +32 2 512 29 21
commechezsoi.be
The restaurant was founded in 1926 by Georges Cuvelier, undoubtedly the great granddaddy of today's generation of Brussels chefs. In the 1930s, it moved to its present location, an Art Nouveau house at Place Rouppe. The current chef, Lionel Rigolet, won the prestigious *Gault Millau*'s Belgian Chef of the Year in 2007. It's Lionel and his wife Laurence's day off when we arrive. They invite me over for a glass of champagne and Lionel cooks up a few dishes: foie gras marinated in genever and his ham mousse.

His hospitality is beyond generous. When I ask more about the Belgium farmed caviar he grabs a 100-gram tin from the fridge and opens it, spooning a generous pile straight into my mouth. The eggs are perfect in shape and colour, with a pleasing texture, a satisfying pop and succulent aftertaste that lingers for minutes. Such hospitality sums up this wonderful city.

Hof Van Cleve
Riemegemstraat 1, 9770 Kruishoutem
☎ +32 9 383 58 48
hofvancleve.com
A visit to the best restaurant in Belgium, Peter Goossens' Hof Van Cleve, has to be on the agenda for all foodies. The guy is a perfectionist and a gentleman. With three Michelin stars, this restaurant celebrates its culture and terroir like very few other restaurants can.

Maison Antoine
Place Jourdan 1, 1040 Etterbeek
☎ +32 2 230 54 56
maisonantoine.be
For the best french fries in Brussels, come to this small permanent street stall within the square called Place Jourdan. It's just opposite the Sofitel Hotel, literally a five-minute drive from the city centre. Many atmospheric bars encircle the square, where once you have bought your cone of fries doused in mayonnaise, you can douse yourself in a beer. Just look for the symbol of the french fry on the door. I was hooked at first bite. Twice cooked in pure ox fat, the flavour is like no other fry, and it passes the crunch test with flying colours. There is debate whether the fries cooked in horse fat at Brasserie George are better, but I will let you decide this. *Carbonades*, or in Dutch *stoofvlees*, are also a specialty – delicate pieces of beef braised for hours in beer.

Sea Grill by Yves Mattagne ↓
Rue Fosse aux Loups 47, 1000
☎ +32 2 212 08 00
seagrill.be
Yves Mattagne has been the head chef here for twenty-four years. He bought the restaurant two years ago from the hotel. Some dishes from the previous era are still served, such as the whole sea bass baked in salt or the lobster veloute with the lobster shells pressed at the table in the stunning, antique silver press. The decor is tastefully modern, tables large and well spaced. It is what I would call a proper two-star with a great chef at the helm. Well worth the visit.

Other places of interest

The Sablon Area
Place du Grand Sablon, 1000
☎ +32 2 513 89 40
trabel.com/brussel/brussels-sablon_square.htm
In my opinion a visit to this area, comprising two distinct, equally lovely zones, Petit Sablon and Grand Sablon, is a must. Petit Sablon is where the best eateries are; its large central square is elegant and beautiful, just like the chic neighbourhood surrounding it, with antique shops, unique bookstores, quaint brasseries and all the best chocolate shops. Be sure to walk up the hill of the Petit Sablon to the gothic church built in the fourteenth century. One of the oldest and most magnificent buildings in Brussels.

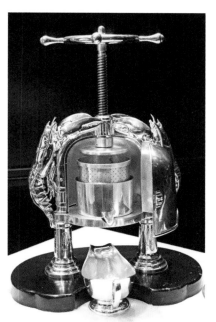

Budapest

We cross beautiful bridges,
try paprika with everything,
and finish off with cake.

Walking across Budapest, you really notice the scale of the place; this is no medieval museum town. It has ambition, it has history, and most of all it has the Danube river. Its central, landlocked position has made it attractive to invaders and conquerors from Mongolia, Turkey, Austria and Russia, all of whom have influenced the food culture.

The Austrian empire ruled Hungary for nearly 400 years. It formed the city layout as we see it today. While Pest is low, flat and built-up, green Buda has hills and gardens – a mix of once-bourgeois residential areas, imposing set-piece castles and churches, and some of the finest cafes and restaurants in the city. Buda looks over Pest and the Danube runs between them; the two parts are connected by many architecturally stunning bridges. The most famous is the Chain Bridge, designed by British architect Adam Clarke and built in the early 1800s. The funds to build the bridge were donated by a nobleman, Istvan Széchenyi. It is the most central of the bridges and leads up to the railway and a stunning road tunnel built around the same time.

The city is recovering from the Iron Curtain era; tradition suffered and food became very basic. It's true that tradition is disappearing from a lot of menus in Budapest but the flipside is that the restaurants that still specialise in Hungarian cuisine have become even more popular, thankfully not with tourists but with locals. They can be hard to find unless you know a local or do extensive research, but I was lucky and had someone to show me around. ➔

1   The Széchenyi Chain Bridge, donated to the city by nobleman Istvan Schéchenyi.
2   The Lion Fountain at Vörösmarty Square.

What is Hungarian cuisine?

Because of my love for Auguste Escoffier, and in turn his love for Hungarian free-range goose and duck liver, I have come to have the romantic notion that this is a specialty of Budapest. I am not disappointed. The other specialties are not well known outside the country's borders; several reasons for this exist. One is that the food is regarded as heavy and high in calories – not true at all. For example there are over a hundred soups for all the seasons. The most well-known and popular is fisherman's soup, normally served as a main course and made of 'sweet water' fish. I love this expression! Mainly small fish are used for the base stock, which is then garnished with carp from the Danube, seasoned paprika and fresh green pepper slices. On special occasions during spring, the soup may be garnished with freshly salted carp roe. Cherry paprika is used on everything. I also tried small, fine pasta sheets garnished with fresh cottage cheese, sour cream, and crispy pork lard pieces.

I talk to Gianni from Pomo d'Oro restaurant and Andras Jokuti, a restaurant critic and food writer/blogger. Andras is as passionate and informative about Hungarian cuisine as it gets. He and I chat for more than an hour about the city. After talking I'm excited. Inevitably, we get round to discussing the definition of what a goulash is. Written gulyás in Hungarian, it is often thought of by Westerners as a spicy rich stew, but that is not quite right. Hungarians view it as a thick soup cooked with some diced meat, usually beef from the leg (silverside), a lot of onions, a few chopped carrots, and new potatoes. It is usually garnished with chopped parsley and little gnocchi-type dumplings. →

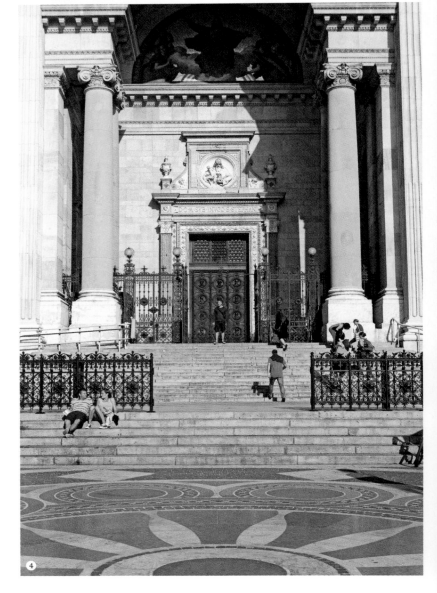

3   A favourite with tourists, this bronze policeman statue's belly is shiny from being rubbed for luck.

4   The Basilica of St Stephen.

Other dishes have evolved from the goulash, such as *paprikasa*, pieces of braised meat, mostly chicken or pork, cooked the same way and traditionally finished with a small amount of sour cream and served with a boiled egg noodle called *nokedli*, similar to *Spätzle*. Another dish popular at most traditional eateries is *pörkölt*, a meat dish made of braised beef or pork, onion, potatoes, and local vegetables. Norbert Jécsy, Miele's managing director, says it is very different to goulash and is made more simply, with larger cuts of meat and less cooking liquor. Onions and paprika are the mainstay and no sour cream is used. It is revered by the Hungarians the way Italians revere pizza.

The choice of sweets is endless. Cakes, confectionery and desserts are normally enjoyed in cafes. Acacia honey is used widely as an ingredient and as a sweetener; it is also the most popular topping on sweet brioche-type bread at breakfast. I do have to admit I have never tasted better honey on my travels. A lot of the upmarket Austrian empire-era cafes were wiped out in the Communist years, so I discover, not to my surprise, that coffee is something the older generation don't normally consume. It is making a resurgence, however, becoming popular amongst young people. Instead, try a shot of *palinka*, a traditional Hungarian type of schnapps. It's a very spicy and aromatic fruit brandy, made from seasonal fruits such as apricots. It can be blended and distilled from the pulp of mixed fruits but for the resulting product to be called *palinka*, they have to originate from fresh and cannot be imported. I love knowing that what I'm drinking came from the lands around me. I am even offered a shot by the chef, Alexandre, after we've finished preparing for the dinner. Someone has to keep up a chef's reputation. →

5   Paprika – fresh, dried or powdered and tinned – is practically a national obsession for the Hungarians.

6   Just a small selection of Hungary's famous sausages (which of course contain paprika).

The wine of Hungary

Many of us know and have tasted the famous Hungarian tokay. The tokay appellation is a blend of *furmint* with *hárslevelű*. Intense and sweet, this wine is one of my favourites.

Wine varieties to look for

Furmint is the white wine grown around Somló, native to the region and similar to chenin blanc in style but with a richer palate, intense yet restrained on the nose. This grape variety will put Hungarian dry white wines on the map internationally over the next few years.

Blaufränkisch is the most important red grape variety; it's similar to merlot with a cabernet franc structure. Depending on the wine-making style, this wine is made to drink young but when well crafted it can age gracefully for twenty years.

Kadarka is generally regarded as cheap wine and there is a lot of rubbish around, but there are some producers now making great *kadarka*. When made with care and understanding and grown under favourable conditions, it's similar to a good pinot noir.

Sparkling wines are very popular and there is a growing industry. Try Louis Francois rose brut NV. For 10€ a bottle this is an absolute bargain.

Any dry white wine from the Somló region is a must, especially wines that have received some old oak treatment. ➜

7　The Basilica of St Stephen.
8　A statue of the Turul, a bird from Hungarian myth, looking out over the city from its majestic perch on the railing of Buda Castle.

Budapest by night

Heroes' Square is worth the journey, either by car or, for the more adventurous, on foot, travelling east up the widest, flashiest boulevard in Budapest, Andrássy út, known as 'The Champs-Elysees of Budapest'. The street finishes when you reach a very large, minimalist square surrounded by some of the most dramatic, beautiful buildings I've ever seen. To the west is a stunning castle and lake that hosts ice skating in winter, and the national gallery is also here. Magnificent bronze statues depict the head of each clan that ruled the lands of Hungary more than 1200 years ago. There is also a very large monument to Stephen the 1st, the first documented King of Hungary, who led the Hungarian nation to Christianity; today this is linked to the national holiday of 20 August, which celebrates King Stephen and is a celebration of the day the first constitution was created. Travel back down Andrássy út to the Danube, over the bridge and up to the Communist monument to freedom. Most locals hate this statue and cannot work out why it's still standing, but it does make a striking landmark. You can fight with other tourists for the best vantage point for looking at the incredible lights of Pest.

Did you know?

'Hungarikum' is the word used to describe a local product from the country that is uniquely Hungarian. Never use this to describe a person from Hungary. ●

9   The bar at Bistro Déryné.
10   Champagne cocktails at Divin Porcello.
11   The magical view of Budapest at night.
12   Heroes' Square, featuring magnificent statues of heroes from Hungarian history.

Fisherman's soup

Serves 4

Known as 'halaszle', this is a famous spicy fish soup made with paprika. Soup is a huge part of the food culture in Hungary, with over 100 different varieties available, but it is not something generally enjoyed by young people. 'Eating and appreciating soup only comes with age', I was reliably informed by my Hungarian contact 'Norbert'.

2 × 1 kg whole fish (try carp, murray cod, catfish, perch or pike)
⅓ cup (80 ml) olive oil
⅓ cup (20 g) sweet smoked paprika
2 medium brown onions, peeled, cut in half and thinly sliced
2 large overripe beef tomatoes, roughly chopped
2 large red capsicums (peppers), roughly chopped (but don't remove the seeds)
2 litres water
sea salt and freshly ground black pepper
lemon juice, to taste
2 green or yellow capsicums (peppers), seeds and membrane removed, cut into 5 mm thick slices
hot potato bread, to serve (use crusty bread if unavailable)
1 whole fresh hot paprika pepper, thinly sliced into rings (optional)

Fillet 1 of the fish, reserving the fillets and chopping them into bite-sized pieces. Chop the carcass and remaining whole fish into large chunks, including the bones and heads with the eyes removed.

Preheat the oven on intensive bake to 200°C.

Heat 2 tablespoons olive oil in a large ovenproof saucepan over medium–high heat, add the chopped fish (except the reserved fillet pieces) and paprika and cook until fragrant. Heat the remaining olive oil in a separate saucepan over medium heat and cook the onion, tomato and red capsicum for about 5 minutes or until softened. Add to the papika and fish mixture, then pour in the water and bring to a simmer. Cover the pan with foil and then a lid and transfer to the oven for 50 minutes.

Remove the pan from the oven and place over an induction set on 6. Simmer for 10 minutes or until the fat of the fish starts to render and rise to the top. At this stage the fish bones should be nice and soft.

Pass the soup through a mouli or potato ricer, then return to a clean pan and bring to a simmer. Add the reserved fish fillet portions and simmer gently for about 10 minutes or until cooked through. Season to taste with salt, pepper and lemon juice.

Garnish with a few capsicum slices and serve with hot bread and chopped paprika pepper rings (if using).

Stuffed cabbage

Serves 4

This is regarded as the Hungarian equivalent of sauerkraut and is generally eaten after midnight to help soak up the alcohol. Although it is mostly made in the home, stuffed cabbage is also found at traditional restaurants. I love the taste of this dish and would order it any time I know it is going to be good. My only complaint is that it doesn't look as delicious as it tastes, so I have added some sauteed cabbage leaves and fresh mint to bring an old classic into the modern world.

2 tablespoons chicken fat or olive oil
2 medium brown onions, finely chopped
2 cloves garlic, finely chopped
3 bay leaves
350 g pork mince
350 g beef mince
½ cup (55 g) finely chopped pancetta
2 tablespoons sweet or hot paprika
½ teaspoon freshly ground black pepper
350 ml tomato juice
1 cup (220 g) cooked basmati rice,
4 large eggs, boiled, peeled and
roughly chopped
1 cup (150 g) drained sauerkraut
sea salt
1 small savoy cabbage, green leaves only,
blanched in boiling water for 1 minute
mint leaves, to garnish
½ cup (120 g) sour cream

Heat the fat or olive oil in a large saucepan over medium heat. Add the onion, garlic and bay leaves and cook until the onion is soft but not coloured. Add the pork, beef and pancetta and cook, stirring to break up any lumps, for about 10 minutes or until the meat is cooked through and crumbly in texture.

Stir in the paprika and pepper, then add the tomato juice and simmer for a further 5 minutes over low heat.

Remove from the heat and add the cooked rice, egg and sauerkraut. Season to taste with salt.

Place the cabbage leaves on individual plates or a platter. Spoon 1 tablespoon of the mixture into each cabbage cup and garnish with mint leaves. Serve warm with a dollop of sour cream.

Sour cherry soup with meringue and blueberries

Serves 4

Cherries here and around the Bavarian basin are like no other I have ever tried. They are not overly large, nor overly sweet, but when fresh they have an incredible aroma that is more than matched by their flavour. Locals combine them with a little sweet and sour cream to make a soup, which is served very simply in a bowl. I have taken the idea and jazzed it up a little.

150 g blueberries
4 cups (600 g) cherries, pitted
½ cup (60 g) almond meal
1 teaspoon ground cinnamon
2 pinches of ground cloves
pinch of sea salt
½ cup (125 ml) port
½ cup (125 g) egg whites
⅓ cup (75 g) caster sugar

Preheat the oven on drying mode to 55°C.

Place the blueberries on a non-stick baking tray and place in the oven for 2 hours. This will 'blister' them, concentrating the flavour and giving a firmer texture. You can do this a few hours ahead, if liked.

An hour before you want to serve, prepare the cherry soup. If you make it any earlier the cherries will oxidise and turn an awful brown colour. Place the cherries, almond meal, cinnamon, cloves, sea salt and port in a high-speed blender or food processor and blend for 5 minutes or until smooth. No need to strain it. Cover and keep it in the fridge until needed.

Place the egg whites in an electric mixer fitted with the whisk attachment. Whisk on high speed until soft peaks form. Do not, under any circumstances, stop the machine during this time otherwise the peaks will drop. Add the sugar and whisk for a further 5 minutes or until it is shiny and the texture of marshmallow.

Spoon the meringue into a piping bag with a plain nozzle and pipe 3 × 5 cm rounds onto the base of each bowl. Add a tablespoon of berries to each serve, then carefully pour 1 cup (250 ml) of cold soup down the side of each bowl so as not to disturb the piped meringue. Serve immediately.

Visitor tips

Cafes

Bistro Déryné ↓
1013 Budapest, Krisztina tér 3
☎ +36 1 225 1407
bistroderyne.com
This fine cafe, bar and brasserie was established in 1914. Between the First and Second World Wars it was the place to be, and it still has a feeling of the period. There's a huge central bar and a lot of little nooks and crannies that wind their way round the space. I recommend the Hungarian breakfast, which consists of several sausages; in particular, *paraszt kolbász*, a type of dark spicy sausage, is really tasty. It's a great place to learn a little bit about Hungarian wine, as you can taste by the glass from the extensive list on the chalk board. All pastries and breads are made on the premises.

Cafe Gerbeaud
1051 Budapest, Vörösmarty tér 7
☎ +36 1 429 9000
gerbeaud.hu
Gerbeaud, established in 1858, is an institution; some locals say it is the most famous *cukrászda* (pastry shop) in Budapest. It dominates Vorosmarty Square, and is apparently the largest cafe in Europe. The most famous cake is *Eszterhazy torta*, a layered almond sponge cake with hazelnut cream.

Central Cafe
1053 Budapest, Károlyi Utca 9
☎ +36 1 266 2110
centralkavehaz.hu
I love the faded splendour of this place, open every day until midnight, on Károlyi Mihály Street. Sitting in the wood-panelled interior, it is easy to imagine eavesdropping on bearded revolutionaries, artists and poets. Art Deco lights hang in high-ceilinged rooms with beautiful painted mouldings and dark wood floors. The waiters act slightly aloof, as though they carry the weight of history around on their trays of cakes and hearty breakfasts.

Művész Cafe
1061 Budapest, Andrássy út 29
☎ + 36 1 343 3544
muveszkavehaz.hu
Művész Cafe is a little out of the way from most of the hotels but if you are taking a stroll up to the Grand Square and the statue of King Steven, then it's worth dropping in here for a snack or cake and coffee.

Coffee

Espresso Embassy
1051 Budapest, Arany János utca 15
☎ +36 30 864 9530
espressoembassy.hu
Yes, you can get a good cup of coffee in this city. Espresso Embassy make great espresso and brewed single origin in a small, intimate space that is nicely decked out. The other great place is My Little Melbourne and there's also a coffee van that pops up around the Kapinski Hotel and nearby parks.

Hotels

Four Seasons 'Gresham Palace'
Széchenyi István tér 5–6, 1051
☎ +36 1 268 6000
fourseasons.com/budapest
The palace is one of the most graceful Art Nouveau buildings in the city, and is in a central spot, in the square on the Pest side of the famous Chain Bridge. At night its lights are breathtaking; walk across the bridge to Adam Clark Square, on the Buda side, and look back to admire the palace. The lobby is grand and luxurious but that said, this hotel is missing something; standard rooms are just that.

Kempinski Hotel
Erzsébet tér 7–8, 1051
☎ +36 1 429 3777
kempinski.com/en/budapest
Great hotel that is really well positioned.
Quite modern, with a vibrant bar and
within walking distance of most of the good
restaurants. Room rates vary but patience
on the internet will get you a great-value
rate, under 200€ for a standard room.

Zenit Budapest Palace Hotel
1052 Budapest, Apáczai Csere János
utca 7
☎ +36 1 799 8400
budapest.zenithoteles.com
A good simple hotel that has some smart
modern design in a fantastic location.
Rates are very good on the internet.

Jogging in Budapest

A must for jogging lovers is to run along
the banks of the Danube. Start at the Pest
side of the chain bridge and cross over to
Buda, run for three kilometres, then cross
over the Margit bridge. Halfway along the
bridge there's a place where you can get
to Margaret Island, an oasis of trees and
manicured gardens, sporting pitches and
playgrounds in the middle of the city. There
is a jogging path around the island – make
sure you only run anti-clockwise; you will
get very grumpy looks if you run clockwise,
as I found out first-hand! The other option
is a quaint path that splits the park down
the middle, so you can run through the
trees. Halfway through are very old public
baths and a more recent addition, a water
park. The baths have a thermal heated pool
so you can stop for a relaxing soak. Then
head back, refreshed, to the north part of
the island to see the small Japanese garden,
and cross over here back to the Pest side
using Arpad Bridge.

Markets

Central Market Hall, Nagy Vasarcsarnok
Vamhaz korut 1-3, Budapest 1093
☎ +36 1 366 3300
piaconline.hu
Why not 'do as the Romans do' and visit
this essential part of everyday life in Pest?
What I love most about it is its grand
space and the profusion of fresh and dried
paprika. I also love that all the vegetables
are local – no imported foods. It is also
cheap. Fresh cherry paprika is 60c a kilo!
The poultry stalls sell every part of the bird:
feet, necks, wings and innards, all displayed
in big, well-presented bays. The market is
buzzing with life but incredibly stylish,
and has a sense of grandiose opulence.

Pubs

Kehli Vendéglő →
1036 Budapest, Mókus utca 22
☎ +36 1 368 0613
kehli.hu
The traditional and atmospheric Kehli, in
the suburb of Obuda, is a bit of a drive along
the Danube, approximately two kilometres
past Margaret Island. Make sure to book
the main room for the live music, or the
tables in the courtyard that look into
the main room. The menu is large and
informative. Fisherman's soup is a must,
garnished with the most delicious fatty
carp and accompanied by some fiery sliced
green peppers. Sauteed duck liver with
onions and sliced peppers are delicious,
not too fatty but still intensely rich.
These livers are free range and are not
classified as foie gras but I found the
taste very similar.

Ruin Pubs
ruinpubs.com
As the name suggests, these are essentially
drinking establishments set up in disused
buildings, often in the courtyards of
derelict apartment blocks – originally
just for summer but some are now open
year-round. They're renowned for their
cheap beer, hip music and interesting
surroundings. Hunt them down simply by
wandering the back streets of Budapest.

Restaurants

Borkonyha Wine Kitchen
1051 Budapest, Sas utca 3
☎ +36 1 266 0835
borkonyha.hu

One of Budapest's most lauded restaurants. It's simple and casual, and one could almost describe it as a wine bar. I would say that anyone interested in Hungarian wine must eat here. The food is for the most part good. You can order wine by the glass and some of the shortcomings on the food side are made up very easily by the atmosphere and dedication to wine service.

Otkerk Bar and Restaurant ↓
1051 Budapest, Zrínyi utca 4
☎ +36 70 330 8652
otkert.hu

A good hangout opposite the Four Seasons, this is where the young and beautiful usually start their night. A great outdoor terrace during the warmer months, live music that is not too intrusive, wide selection of beers and some good casual food. The prices here are so cheap.

Trattoria Pomo d'Oro →
1051 Budapest, Arany János utca 9
☎ +36 1 302 6473
pomodorobudapest.com

Gianni Annoni is an Italian made good in Budapest. He is a star of *Masterchef* who has lived in the city for seventeen years and started a restaurant and importing business, bringing in high-quality meats, oils, cheeses and wines from Italy. To say this guy is a real character is an understatement. He knows everybody; they stop their Range Rovers in the middle of the street to shake his hand, with cars tooting ferociously behind them, only to pull up and do the same themselves! He's young, passionate and energetic, which translates to his restaurants, particularly Pomo d'Oro, which is regarded as one of the best in Hungary. He takes us from the restaurant to his apertivo bar Divin Porcello, where vibrant locals enjoy complimentary snacks with the spritzers.

Italian restaurants are an established part of the Budapest food culture, dating back to the Polgary period. Gianni's food is simple and relies on fresh market visits every morning. A visit here is a must.

Trams

The Most Scenic Tram Ride in Europe
The journey followed by Budapest's #2 tram was voted the most scenic in Europe by *National Geographic* magazine; it is an accolade of which Budapest's natives are proud, but one that many feel only confirms what they already know. The ride begins at the south terminus in a normal, rather underwhelming city landscape, which adds to the drama and the sense of expectation even more, then trundles past the cultural complex next to Rákóczi Bridge, and then from there the scenery and architecture leave you in no doubt about where you are and why you are here.

Byron Bay

A famously laid-back town, where we
soak up the sunshine and visit one of
the best farmers' markets in Australia.

No other town juxtaposes the old and new culture of Australia more seamlessly than Byron Bay, or 'Byron' as it is affectionately known by anyone who regularly visits. It's located on the most easterly point of mainland Australia, where lush rainforest competes with the pastoral perfection of the hinterlands, sweeping majestically down to the ocean, at once a raging clash of the elements and a serene Pacific idyll. And the beaches . . . the perfect place for sandcastles and a paddle, or the ultimate surf, its consistent breaks attract hundreds of serious surfers each year. European settlement of Byron runs all the way back to 1770, when Captain Cook used the bay to anchor during rough weather. He named the area Cape Byron after John Byron. It wasn't until the late 1960s that Byron Bay evolved into the relaxed tourist destination it is today. The town is currently home to close to 5000 locals, but you can multiply that number by five come holiday season.

Something happens to people when they cross the Byron city limits; some mystical, omniscient power calls forth one's inner hippy, as though everyone who visits is auditioning for a role in the musical *Hair*. No shoes, no make-up, tanned healthy bodies and a tendency to spurt out the occasional 'No worries, mate' become mandatory. Despite being burdened with the most uninspiring, inactive council in Australia's 200-hundred year history, resulting in poor roads, poor traffic, unmanaged coastal erosion, erratic house prices and small businesses being forced to operate under heavy bureaucratic scrutiny with little confidence, the town still seems to have the Australian spirit in abundance. The most successful, wealthiest captain of industry and the most laidback larrikin will sit side by side with a pot of beer and talk for hours, or compare fishing tips over a pulled pork bun at what I consider to be the best farmers' market in Australia, operating every Thursday morning. The 'back to nature' approach is the secret behind the great produce, and the sensational weather doesn't hurt. Let's just say you won't see ➔

1–2   The beach at Byron Bay. Despite being a popular tourist destination, there are still plenty of secluded spots.

3   Dr Markus Miele took some time out to reflect during the weekend in Byron Bay that the last time he was here he was on his honeymoon with his wife Katya.

4   The town is also close to accessible rainforest, with plenty of easy walks.

tomatoes here in the middle of August; instead there's fresh lemongrass, fragrant yuzu citrus and organically grown, grass-fed beef. Byron's organic market is a microcosm of food culture on the east coast of Australia. No other market in either Sydney or Brisbane typifies what it means to be a 'local' farmer better than this one, and the people who sell their produce here are truly living the dream.

Miele has a close relationship with Harvey Norman so there are no better people to ask for their opinion on Australian food culture. We organise to meet up with Katie Page and her husband Gerry Harvey, along with my mate and butcher Anthony Puharich and his gorgeous wife Rebecca. Anthony has created what is undoubtedly the most opulent butchery in Australia – Victor Churchill in Woollahra, Sydney. The boutique premises celebrate quality meat. Anthony believes that at its finest, meat is an item of luxury we can enjoy every day, something to be savoured and respected.

Katie and Gerry have generously invited us to stay the weekend with them on their glorious property at Byron at Byron resort. Located on the southern outskirts of town with a rainforest walk through to Tallows Beach, where the lush tropics gird the shoreline, the venue is a world-class resort. I don't know how many millions have been invested in this project, converting mosquito-infested swampland into sustainable, eco-friendly villas, but they should be applauded.

Byron brings me back to what life is all about – food, fabulous food! Saturday morning is the famed Bangalow farmers' market. We all decide that is where we will start the day and I have promised Katie that I'll cook dinner that night. We have no idea what the menu will be but I'm determined that it all has to be local. Cory Campbell, chef at Vue du Monde, loves Byron so I have brought him up for some sun and surf, and my better half, Madeleine, somehow manages to drop filming and our four kids for the weekend. It's her first break in about six months so she's more than happy to come along for a feed, and the promise of a sleep-in. The market is small but truly a fair dinkum farmers' market. I even have trouble understanding the vegetable grower; he doesn't speak English, he speaks 'Strine'! ➜

5   The Byron and Bangalow farmers' markets are among the best in the country.
6   Gerry Harvey enjoying the seasonal red delicious apples at Byron Farmers' Market.

The third week of August in Melbourne is always a bleak one, weather-wise. Bone-chillingly cold, biting wind and rain with top temperatures of around 16 degrees. Byron is completely different – blue sky and the temperature tops out at about 24 degrees. It doesn't just feel like a different state, it's like a different planet! Not bad for winter.

So what does this mean for produce? Simply put, it means that there is a lot more to choose from. Even the apple season is different. The last of the red delicious are still being sold at the market. John Sing is the region's most celebrated pig farmer and has helped put free-range Bangalow Pork on the menu of nearly every restaurant in Australia. He is passionate about saving rare breeds such as the Japanese Black Kurobuta, also known as the Black Berkshire. We buy a rack and a belly off him for the evening's feast.

This sort of attitude towards the way we should look at produce has brought about some interesting changes to the community, especially in Bangalow. Its market is the largest regular community gathering every Saturday in the long history of the town. When the Catholic church shut up shop ten years ago, the markets came to restore a sense of community, bringing the venerable residents of Bangalow together. The general manager of the Byron and Bangalow farmers' markets proudly explains, 'It has kept this town on the map.'

Gerry, Katie and Markus are soon locked in a passionate discussion, allowing me the opportunity to press my point home regarding the need for goods to be more regional, tell more of a story on the plate, and that we need to be prepared to pay more for them. Katie, extremely knowledgeable and perceptive, points out that Australians have an appetite for cheaper products and don't all share my philosophy, making my vision a real challenge. She says Australia's dollar will be the saviour: as it drops back to realistic values, consumers will have to accept that buying cherries from California in our winter is just simply unacceptable on so many levels and they will have to accept the 'terrible' notion of seasons. Including my old man, who insists on buying his grandkids strawberries from the Victoria market in the middle of June! ➔

7–8   The bakery at Harvest.
9   Meat hanging in the Harvest provedore shop, where it is available to buy.

Walking around the market doesn't take long as there are only, I would say, twenty stalls. But they are all different. There's a bit of everything, from Noel and his locally farmed rock oysters to freshly churned butter made in the Byron hinterland, washed-rind cheeses to grass-fed beef, and hard-boiled lollies to macadamia nuts.

Amid so much incredible produce, the menu quickly starts to come together in my head. The grass-fed beef has an incredible rich red colour and looks wonderfully firm. Thankfully it is not packaged in the now-mandatory horrible vacuum bags that leave the meat limp and lifeless. A tartare with finely grated daikon and thinly sliced cayenne chillies will make a great start.

Dessert has to involve some of the local macadamia nuts, and the Bangalow cheese company's great milk and cream. The morning moves quickly; Gerry is a fascinating guy, a man in his mid-seventies who has given everything to his three passions: creating one of the best retail store chains in the world; horse racing and stud breeding; and pastoral farming in a sustainable and ethical way. He is forthright with his opinions but also a great listener, very humble and down to earth. All that passion works up an appetite; perfect time for a coffee and scone at Harvest Cafe and General Store in Newrybar. Resembling an old settlers' shack, Harvest has been lovingly restored into a bustling cafe with great coffee. I simply adore this place. It is everything I'm passionate about in great cafes: casual but with cleverly thought-out design and a location that is as Australian as it gets. It serves first-class produce simply, and the staff are great – one of my former chefs, Josh Lewis, amongst them! He generously supplies us with some perfectly ripe custard apples. Just another example of the generosity so evident in these parts. ➜

10   Harvest serves locally grown produce and excellent coffee.
11   A sunny afternoon at Bayleaf cafe.

The afternoon is bathed in glorious sunshine, perfect to get us in the mood to cook. Cory has one more mission to complete; he knows a local fisherman whom he has texted, organising some fresh prawns, swordfish fillets and yellowfin tuna, all in season and all line-caught. He drives off to pick it up and I crack on with some prep at the villa. My chef Brandon, meanwhile, borrows the kitchen of the Byron at Byron resort to whip up a 'show-stopper dessert'. His words, and he refuses to tell me what he is doing! All the brief I gave him was to ensure he includes the custard apple and I suggest that something with limes and associated fragrant herbs, such as lime curd with lemongrass, will go well.

Dusk swiftly falls and the ad hoc menu has come together nicely, boasting some really interesting dishes, all inspired by the local *terroir*. Cory and I were a little apprehensive about serving Katie and Gerry food that was too complicated, simply because they are people who eat out a lot and all they requested was conversation with friends and good food. I'll just mention that it's bloody hard cooking and conversing. So much so I burnt the rack of pork! Quick thinking by Cory and we make a master stock with what is in the cupboard and braise the back-up pork belly. The evening saved. Gerry, Anthony and I work out a plan to save the paddock-to-plate industry by designing and rolling out portable abattoirs that process the animals on the farm rather than taking them to much larger abattoir plants that stress them, affecting quality. I get so excited about the idea I end up emailing Lyn White from Animals Australia, the brave person who exposed the live cattle trade and showed how cruel the trade can be overseas. The response is positive – they have begun building a prototype. The night finishes late; that is all I remember. Madeleine and I come away with the notion that we are pretty lucky to meet and be with the people around the table that night.

Next morning there is time for a quick walk along Tallows, where we spot the most amazing whale jump a few hundred metres out to sea. It was one of those moments that if you didn't see it yourself, you'd never believe it. I'm so lucky to call this country home. ●

12   Patricia Jeanes with coffee and scones at Harvest.

13–14 An outdoor lunch followed by a walk along the beach – there's no more Australian way to spend an afternoon.

Simple raw tuna wrapped in lettuce

Serves 5

Big eye tuna belly is in abundance around the far-north coast of New South Wales. The freshness of this magnificent fish is best appreciated by eating it raw. This is the modern Australian way of eating and is finally being accepted as not sashimi, but great picnic and barbecue food!

100 g yellowfin tuna fillet (the freshest possible), cleaned and cut into 5 mm dice
splash of olive oil
30 small sprigs dill, washed and patted dry
finely grated zest and juice of 2 limes
sea salt
15 baby cos lettuce leaves, washed and patted dry
30 rocket or nasturtium flowers, washed and patted dry

Mix the tuna with the olive oil, then refrigerate until needed.

Just before serving, mix the tuna with the dill sprigs and lime zest, and add salt and lime juice to taste. Place a pile of the tuna mixture on each leaf and garnish with 2 rocket or nasturtium flowers per serve.

The classic Aussie beetroot salad

Serves 4

I am positive that we Aussies consume more beetroot than the Russians. We have to! In my own gardens we have 3 seasons of beetroot and I always have it represented on my menu somewhere. Similarly, it went straight on the menu here after I shopped at the Bangalow markets, where I found the biggest, meatiest beetroot I'd ever seen. Such a delicious vegetable – no barbecue is complete without it.

4 large beetroot, well washed
1½ tablespoons apple vinegar
100 ml olive oil
finely grated zest of 1 lemon
sea salt
100 g soft fresh goat's cheese, crumbled
20 mustard leaves (or use rocket leaves)

Preheat the steamer to 100% steam. Add the beetroot and cook for 25 minutes or until tender. Remove and allow to cool slightly. While still warm, rub off the beetroot skin using your fingers (you may want to use prep gloves for this). Thinly slice the beetroot or cut it into bite-sized pieces, then place in a non-metallic bowl with the apple vinegar, olive oil, lemon zest and salt. Leave to marinate for 10 minutes.

Divide the beetroot and marinade among 4 plates, sprinkle the goat's cheese and mustard leaves over the top and serve.

Masterstock braised pork belly with dill potatoes

Serves 4

Great Australian chef Cheong Liew inspired my generation of cooks to always keep a masterstock in the fridge, ready for those days when a piece of pork belly screamed to be poached until silky and soft, with the fragrance of a Malay hawker market. The modern accompaniment to this is potato salad! Now we're talking.

If you look after it, a masterstock can last for years. Simply strain and boil it after every use and refrigerate it correctly, then top it up with more stock before using it next time. The flavour will become unique to your kitchen.

800 g piece free-range pork belly

Masterstock
2 cups (500 ml) dark soy
2 cups (500 ml) light soy
½ cup (125 ml) shaoxing cooking wine
1 litre chicken stock
6 star anise
2 cinnamon sticks
2 small pieces cassia bark
2 tablespoons crushed palm sugar
4 cloves garlic, peeled and thinly sliced
**60 g knob of ginger, peeled and very
    thinly sliced**
8 spring onions, green ends only
4 pieces dried tangerine peel, sliced

Dill potatoes
**500 g royal blue or kipfler potatoes, washed
    and cut into 1 cm thick slices**
sea salt
good handful of dill, roughly chopped
100 g cultured butter

Preheat the oven on the conventional setting to 160°C.

To make the masterstock, place all the ingredients in a large saucepan and bring to the boil.

Place the pork in a deep baking tray. Pour the hot stock all over the pork, then cover with a lid (or a few layers of foil) and place in the oven. Braise for 3–4 hours or until tender. For best results, leave the pork in the stock and refrigerate overnight. The next day, reheat the pork in the stock, cut it into thick slices and serve. The stock can be strained, refrigerated and reused.

For the dill potatoes, place the potato slices in a single layer in a wide-based saucepan, cover with water and season well with salt. Add the dill and bring to the boil, then reduce the heat and simmer for 5–8 minutes or until the potato is just tender but still has a crunch. Drain and mix with the butter while hot. Season with salt.

Serve with the braised pork belly and, if you like, the Aussie beetroot salad (see page 97).

Visitor tips

Cafes

Bayleaf Cafe ↓
2 Marvell St, Byron Bay 2481
☎ +61 2 6685 8900
Conveniently located in the centre of town, this is the best place in Byron for coffee. The beans are sourced and roasted by previous owner Miko, and new owner Dan still liaises daily with him on quality. Coffee is served in many ways and made from several choices of freshly ground beans of different origins. Breakfasts and light lunches using locally sourced produce are their specialities. Avocado, poached eggs, tomato and chilli salsa on crisp flatbread is a winner.

Doma Japanese Cafe in Federal
3–6 Albert St, Federal
☎ +61 2 6688 4711
The best Japanese food on the NSW coast. Hand rolls made to order, great coffee and Japanese sweets. Try the crispy chicken hand roll. Buy some cold beers from the general store next door and sit on the fixed benches outside in the park or in the old classroom turned dining room. There is something so right about this cafe. It simply sums up the modern Australia.

Downtown Cafe (Bangalow)
33 Byron Street, Bangalow 2479
☎ +61 2 6687 2555
townbangalow.com.au
Small and bustling with great cakes, sandwiches and coffee, this cafe is packed from morning to night. Any cake created by Katrina and her team is recommended.

Harvest ↓
18–20 Old Pacific Highway, Newrybar
☎ +61 2 6687 2644
harvestcafe.com.au
Without a doubt the best all-round cafe/restaurant on the north coast, 5 minutes' drive out of Byron on the Pacific Highway (see also the listing for Uptown, this page). The cafe consists of a large indoor–outdoor dining space serving breakfast and lunch, seven days, with dishes such as grilled Australian snapper with herb sauce and beetroot greens. All bread is baked on-site, and on Saturdays the bread oven is open to the public. A large table full of sourdoughs, simple cakes and pastries for locals to try is on display. First in, first served.

The Top Shop
65 Carlyle Street, Byron Bay 2481
☎ +61 2 6685 6495
What looks like a residential house on
the southern outskirts of town towards
Wategos is the best burger joint in Byron.
They have only a take-away licence to serve
the hordes of locals and tourists drawn to
the simple yet well-executed menu and
excellent coffee, but it's a great experience
just sitting on the front lawn of the house,
soaking up the early afternoon sun.

Markets

Byron Farmers' Markets →
Butler St, Byron Bay 2481
☎ +61 2 6680 9703
byronfarmersmarket.com.au
In my opinion, the most authentic farmers'
market in Australia, every Thursday
morning. It has some very special food
stands: everything from vegan samosas to
pulled pork buns is served for a decadent
breakfast as you walk around fantasising
about what you're going to create for
dinner out of such amazing seasonal
produce. Also check out the market every
Saturday morning in nearby Bangalow
(www.bangalowmarket.com).

Resort

The Byron at Byron
77–97 Broken Head Road, 2481
☎ +61 2 6639 2000
thebyronatbyron.com.au
Set in the middle of the rainforest, this
place is a true retreat from the stresses of
the world. It's an easy walk to the beach
and just five minutes' drive from town, and
each suite has its own kitchen for those
evenings when you'd rather stay in.

Restaurant

Uptown (Bangalow)
33 Byron Street, Bangalow, 2479
☎ +61 2 6687 2555
townbangalow.com.au
Uptown restaurant is owned and operated
by one of Australia's most skilled pastry
chefs, Katrina Kanetani, with her husband
Karl. They serve a six-course degustation
three nights a week, serving fresh seasonal
produce with a leaning towards seafood
and the hinterland's famous pork farms.
The execution is world class and the
restaurant is in the heart of the prettiest
Art Deco town in the Byron hinterland.

Dubai

A city of riches, where exotic
silks and spices contrast with
space-age buildings.

Dubai is a beast of a city; its relentless expansion seems impossible to stop. If you compare photos from the early 1990s with recent ones, the rapid transformation is hard to believe – eight-lane highways and buildings more than a hundred stories high. Many find it irresistible, lured by tax-free dollars and the promise of warm weather and its associated lifestyle. I can tell you from first-hand experience that these factors lose their gloss quite quickly. Ever tried jogging along a beach when it is 34°C at 6 a.m.?

Dubai was once a city of Bedouin camps trading with the Far East. I'm not in search of lost food recipes or 'authentic' restaurants; I'm in search of what people are eating right now. One of my first-ever apprentice chefs, Tom Arnel, who worked for me for well over six years, is now a resident here in Dubai, about to open his first cafe operation. There is no better person to guide me through the maze of luxury and the carefully orchestrated facade designed by Dubai's founding fathers to cloud some harsher realities. People come here to escape reality; this is the only city in the world with no unemployment! That is right: no working visa, no residency! A population of 10 million people, 90 per cent expats, 10 per cent locals, and all of them receiving income means one thing: everybody can eat out.

Well-known chefs, restaurateurs and hoteliers only open in Dubai for one reason: money. There are too many reputable and excellent operators here to mention even one-fifth of them. Operating in such an environment requires a suitably impressive business plan. Quality has to come first. Competition dictates that, and so does the array of professionals who are attracted here for all the same reasons. They expect only the best. Some of these establishments may suffer from lack of soul, but hey, when you are in a desert with lush gardens and a golf course, you can't have everything. →

1 Dubai's incredible skyline looks like something from the future.

2 The old Textile Souk, where traditionally woven and printed fabrics are sold.

There is the side to Dubai I have just mentioned and then there is the side I don't know. Dubai on 100 dirhams a day (AUD$30 a day) is the side I want to know. I love luxury, but as I grow older I want more; I want memories. Cynthia, my host for Dubai, is the most patient person I have ever met. She has made over fifty suggestions for my fleeting 24-hour visit to the city but none of them really grab my attention. It is only when I hit the ground and we get to talk that Cynthia realises what I'm after; her eyes light up and her ever-present smile becomes wider. I know what the wealthy do when they want to dress up but what do they do when they want to dress down?

Breakfast time; most concierges will direct you to the downtown area, Souk al Bahar. There aren't many great Western-style breakfast places in Dubai, so I suggest eating what the local community eat. I would definitely steer clear of Souk al Bahar if you can; it's a tourist mecca, but if you do find yourself in that part of town there is one place I'd recommend. The Pavilion is a great little modern industrial Arabic cafe and art house. The food is nothing special, but there's a great vibe. Alternatively, check out a Palestinian breakfast at Zaroob.

Not surprisingly the Miele launch here was the most glamorous: lavish flower arrangements, butlers from a five-star hotel, rooftop bar, and everyone dressed to impress.

The next step is a tour of the spice souk, the gold souk, the textile souk . . . souks everywhere and funnily enough they are all in Dubai Creek. Having travelled the Middle East extensively, I can tell you that these are not real souks so really, I would recommend you stay away! The culture here is never going to slap you in the face; that is not the point of being here. What you are seeing is change; some say for the better, others not. What I see is a city that doesn't take no for an answer; there is plenty to like with an attitude like that. Just remember that a city in the desert is always best to visit during the cooler months (November to April).

Have you heard of cloud seeding? Well, not only does it happen in Dubai, it is actually government policy. Anything is possible in this city. A plane flies up into the sky and distributes chemicals that create rain clouds. Someone has to turn the desert green! ●

3–9   In the souks – the markets of Dubai, where people come to trade, buy groceries, eat and have henna tattoos done. You can even see fabric dyes in their natural state, such as these rocks of indigo dye.

10–13 Artificial canals and ponds along with lavish interiors in and around The Palm all help to create a sense of opulence.

14   The Royal Saffron, an esteemed spice shop where whole fresh spices can be bought.

15   Classic mint tea, served in delicate glasses.

16   A ferry over Dubai Creek in a traditional Arabic *dhow* (boat).

10

11

12

13

14

15

16

Salted beef with pistachio paste and pickled eggplant

Serves 4

Although the ingredients in the title may not directly remind you of Dubai, they do evoke sophistication and that is what this city strives for every day. This recipe uses Himalayan salt blocks, which are pretty common around the world these days. The heat transfers the salt into the raw beef in a manner not dissimilar to curing. Ask your butcher for the best and freshest beef tenderloin he has, with no oxidised colour. If you don't like pistachios, green olive tapenade is a good alternative.

2 Himalayan salt blocks
**1 large eggplant (aubergine), cut lengthways
    into 8 pieces**
sea salt
1 tablespoon extra virgin olive oil
juice of ¼ lemon
**400 g beef tenderloin, trimmed and cut into
    8 cm × 3 cm pieces about 3 mm thick**
viola flowers and mustard cress, to serve

Pistachio paste
200 g roasted pistachio kernels
2½ tablespoons water
1 tablespoon apple vinegar
sea salt
150 ml grapeseed oil

Pickling liquor
110 ml white wine vinegar
90 g honey
200 ml water

Preheat the oven on intensive bake to 160°C.

Preheat a warmer drawer and place the salt blocks in the centre. Keep them there until they're warm and ready for serving.

To make the pistachio paste, blitz the pistachios in a food processor, adding the water to form a basic puree (don't be too concerned if it is not completely smooth). Add a splash of apple vinegar at a time to taste, then season with salt. Slowly drizzle in the grapeseed oil to emulsify, then taste and season again with salt and vinegar until you are satisfied with the balance of flavours.

To make the pickling liquor, combine all the ingredients in a small saucepan and bring to the boil over high heat. Remove the pan from the heat and leave to cool.

Place the eggplant in a bowl with a good amount of salt, the olive oil and a squeeze of lemon juice. Mix together using your hands and leave to macerate for a few minutes, then transfer to a baking tray and roast for 20 minutes. Remove and allow to cool for up to 15 minutes. Cut each long wedge of eggplant lengthways into 3 pieces and place in the pickling liquor for 20 minutes, then remove. You can prepare this component in advance if you like and store it in the fridge – just bring it back to room temperature before serving.

Remove the salt blocks from the warmer draw. Place the beef flat on the blocks, then spoon some pistachio paste onto each slice of beef and spread with the back of a spoon. Place one piece of pickled eggplant on the end of each piece and finish with flowers and cress.

Serve the beef slices on the salt blocks. Use chopsticks or fingers to roll each piece of beef into a roll, enclosing the filling.

Braised lamb and rice with spices

Serves 4

Machboos is a popular one-pot dish in which meat and onions are seasoned with spices, salt and dried limes (loomi) and cooked in boiling water until very tender. The meat comes out and the rice goes in, and cooks in the richly flavoured braising liquid. The loomi give this dish its authentic flavour so it's definitely worth tracking them down – any African food store will have them.

2½ teaspoons ground turmeric
2½ teaspoons ground cumin
2½ teaspoons curry powder
1½ teaspoons chilli powder (optional)
3 teaspoons ground cinnamon
pinch of saffron threads
2 tablespoons olive oil
1 large onion, cut into 8 pieces
1 large tomato, cut into 8 pieces
5 cloves garlic, minced
2 dried limes (loomi)
3 litres water
2 Knorr chicken bouillon cubes
    (or good-quality chicken stock cubes)
1 × 2 kg lamb leg
sea salt
2 cups (400 g) basmati rice, boiled
    or steamed until tender

Preheat the oven on the conventional setting to 160°C.

Place a large flameproof casserole dish over medium heat, add the spices and toast until fragrant. Remove from the dish and set aside. Pour in the olive oil, add the tomato, onion, garlic and loomi and cook over medium heat for 5 minutes or until the onion starts to separate. Return the spices to the pan, then add the water and stock cubes and bring to the boil. Add the lamb leg and season lightly with salt. Cover with foil and then a tight-fitting lid and bake in the oven for 3 hours.

When the meat is tender enough to fall off the bone with ease, remove the leg from the dish and keep it warm. By this stage the sauce should be nice and thick, not too runny. Stir in the rice, then cover tightly with a fresh piece of foil and the lid and bake for a further 20 minutes. Remove from the oven and rest for 20 minutes without disturbing the foil seal.

Take the dish straight to the table and break the foil seal in front of your guests. Serve the leg on a separate platter for ease of access. Enjoy!

Egg and vermicelli omelette with apricots

Serves 4

Known as 'balaleet' this pleasing combination of sweet vermicelli and hearty omelette is a difficult dish to pigeonhole. In the Gulf it may be eaten as a main course at dinner or served as a dessert, but it is also widely enjoyed for breakfast. In the method below I suggest making 4 individual omelettes but if you don't have the time for this (or a small enough pan), 1 large omelette will be just as good. Just increase the cooking time in the oven to around 6 minutes.

3 eggs, lightly beaten
3 eggs, extra, separated
pinch of saffron strands
2 teaspoons ground cinnamon
1 teaspoon freshly grated nutmeg
½ teaspoon mixed spice
¼ teaspoon rosewater
½ cup (110 g) caster sugar
40 g cultured butter
1 cup vermicelli, soaked for 5–10 minutes
**   until soft, then roughly chopped**
icing sugar, for dusting
4 scoops of vanilla ice-cream
mint sprigs, to garnish

Apricot puree
2 apricots, cut in half, stones removed
caster sugar, for sprinkling

Preheat the oven on intensive bake to 160°C.

To make the apricot puree, place the apricot halves on a small baking tray, cut-side up. Sprinkle with sugar and roast for about 5 minutes or until soft. Remove and cool a little, then peel off the skin and mash with a spoon. Taste and add a little more sugar if you think it needs it. Leave the oven on for the omelettes.

Combine the eggs, extra egg yolks, spices and rosewater in a bowl and whisk for 1 minute.

Place the extra egg whites in an electric mixer fitted with the whisk attachment and whip until soft peaks form. Add the sugar, then beat on high for a further 3 minutes until the meringue is glossy and firm peaks have formed. Immediately fold the meringue into the beaten egg mixture.

Heat an 18 cm frying pan over an induction set on 7 or a gas burner over medium–high heat. Place an egg ring in the pan and melt a quarter of the butter in the ring. Sprinkle an eighth of the vermicelli noodles into the ring and fry for 1 minute. Add a quarter of the egg mixture and carefully spread it over the noodles. Sprinkle over another portion of noodles and cook for 1 minute to set the bottom of the omelette and give it a nice golden colour. Transfer the pan to the oven and cook for 3 minutes.

Remove the omelette from the pan and keep warm while you make the remaining omelettes.

Dust the omelettes with icing sugar and serve with the apricot puree and a scoop of ice-cream. Garnish each serve with a sprig of mint.

Visitor tips

Art galleries

Al Quoz
emirates.com/au/english/
destinations_offers/
discoverdubai/sightseeingindubai/
alquozartgalleries.aspx
While you're grabbing a great coffee in the district of Al Quoz, why not check out the more than thirty art galleries showcasing local artists? You will not find tourists here, only locals and expats wanting to do a little bit of speculating, hunting for the next great up-and-coming artist.

Bars

Armani Lounge
Armani Hotel Dubai, Burj Al Khalifa
☎ +971 4 888 3308
dubai.armanihotels.com
Sometimes you just need a whisky sour or a Rusty Nail. My first stop is the Armani Hotel. Check out the spacious bar on the ground floor that looks out on to the largest water feature in the world; the show begins every half hour on the half hour from 6 p.m. Well worth the $25 cocktail.

The Jetty Lounge
One & Only Royal Mirage, Umm Suqeim
☎ +971 4 399 9999
royalmirage.oneandonlyresorts.com/
cuisine/barsandclubs/jettylounge.aspx
One of the best places for a romantic, relaxed drink on the sand. A frozen margarita goes down well, or if you're after something simpler try an Estrella, one of my favourite beers.

Zuma Restaurant & Bar
Gate Village 06, DIFC
☎ +971 4425 5660
zumarestaurant.com/zuma-landing/
dubai/en/welcome
The local glitterati drink here, and tourists seek out this highly reliable eatery too. This bar's real asset, apart from its style and quality, is its proximity to all the major hotels. Some may find its environment a little clichéd, and be warned, the music on the upper level gets loud and the atmosphere smoky after 10 p.m. Food is always good, though, featuring a mixture of Asian cuisines.

Casual eateries

Bu Qtair Cafeteria
Road 4D, near Burj Al Arab
☎ +971 055 705 2130
This 'fish shack place' near Jumeirah Hotel is pretty much right on the beach. I will swear, not one word of a lie, that the fish I had here was the tastiest piece of local fish I have ever eaten. The concept is simple: no menu, just a tray of marinated whole fish, a tray of prawns, a couple of Indian guys and a chargrill. The food is cheap and served with a bowl of curry sauce and naan bread. One of the simplest

and best food experiences of the trip; the only thing missing was that first sip of an ice-cold beer.

Calicut Pargon
20 B Street, Karamah
☎ +971 4 335 8700
As authentic Keralan Indian food as you can get; I can't recommend it highly enough. It's off the beaten track – only locals go here.

Ravi Restaurant ↓
Al Dhiyafa Road
☎ +971 4 331 5353
Many expats call this Pakistani restaurant the real Dubai. There are no tourists when we visit, though it's only ten minutes in a cab from all the major hotels. Communal tables are shared with mostly men of Pakistani origin. 1970s bathroom tiles on the walls and unbelievable curries, rice dishes and fresh flatbreads. Cutlery is given to Westerners, but it is so much more fun doing what everyone else is doing and using your fingers (right hand only) to dip bread into the lentils and butter chicken. Also try the more family-friendly Ravi Palace next door. Average prices for dishes work out at less than $3 a plate. Try baked chicken on the bone from the tandoor oven, where all the bread is also baked.

Smiling BKK Thai Restaurant ↓
Al Wasl Plaza, Al Wasl Road,
Shop 22, Jumeirah 1
☎ +971 800 8424
A special little 'hole in the wall',
completely hidden away off Al Wasl road,
with the kitchen run by a 75-year-old
Thai lady. The food is good, and it's off
the tourist trail.

Zaroob
Shop # 1, Ground Floor Jumeirah Tower,
Sheikh Zayed Road
☎ +971 4 327 6060
zaroob.com
A cross between Palestinian street food and
fast food. Dinner after 10 p.m. has never
been better. Open all day and night, every
day. I loved this place; who wouldn't when
you can't spend more than $50 for two
people? Breakfast is highly recommended
– eggs cooked in bread with fresh tomato
salads, an array of dips, and freshly
squeezed fruit and vegetable juices.

Coffee

Raw Coffee
Warehouse 10, Cnr 7a & 4a Sts, Al
Manara, Al Quoz
☎ +971 4 339 5474
rawcoffeecompany.com
Matt and Kim, two Kiwis, run one of
only four coffee roasters in Dubai. The
difference with this one is they specialise
in what I call *real* coffee: carefully chosen
single origin beans and blends that are all
freshly roasted and served on the premises.
Set in the back streets of Al Quoz, the
coffee shop is literally a warehouse filled
with hessian sacks of green coffee beans,
blackboards with daily recommendations,
and two La Marzocco coffee machines.
And, of course, some comfy chairs and
tables. For the best coffee in Dubai, this
place is worth scouting out.

Tom & Serg
Al-Joud Center, Al Quoz Area (near Ace
Hardware on Sheikh Zayed Road)
☎ +971 0 56 474 6812
tomandserg.com
Look out for Tom Arnel's first venture after
helping yours truly set up the Jones the
Grocer menus for the Middle East. Tom
loved Dubai so much he stayed, determined
to bring Melbourne's coffee culture there,
along with a well-trained front-of-house
team and fully qualified baristas. Set in the
downtown warehouse district of Souk al
Bahar, this venue is open all day with great
food and coffee.

Hotels

Burj Al Arab
Jumeira 3
☎ +971 4 301 7777
jumeirah.com/Burj-Al-Arab
To sum up the Burj: if you want to visit, stay
a night, otherwise stay away! This is a great
experience but again very touristy; very
glitzy and it's the predictable side of Dubai.

One and Only Resort ←
West Crescent, The Palm
☎ +971 4 440 1010
thepalm.oneandonlyresorts.com
Excellent hotel sitting near the marina
with great beach accessibility amidst the
luxury. All One and Only resorts are top
notch, keeping many a bucket list ticked
off. Tennis courts, beaches, gyms, and plush
rooms with a sense of their location. They
don't come cheap but, hey, you have gone
this far and you're in Dubai so think about
it before you dismiss the idea. You may
even get lucky online!

Produce

Fresh Express Gourmet
☎ +971 4 884 8811
freshexpressint.com
A great gourmet store from the best in the
hospitality supply business. Vice-president
Girard Vouyoukas and his team are
passionate. I know this first-hand as he is
my supplier whenever I work in the Middle
East. House-smoked and cured fish of
different types, as well as pickled olives and
vegetables. Where there is a quality local
producer, Girard will use them; if not, he
will source the best from around the world.

Restaurants

La Petite Maison
Dubai International Financial Center
☎ +971 4 439 0505
lpmdubai.ae
Many local expats regard this as the best
food in Dubai. Worth visiting for lunch.

Reflets by Pierre Gagnaire
InterContinental Dubai Festival City,
Festival Boulevard
☎ +971 4 701 1111
pierre-gagnaire.com/#/reflets/
ambiance_reflets
Not cheap, but a gastronomic experience
nonetheless, and one of the best in Dubai.

Restaurant Gary Rhodes
Le Royal Meridien Beach Resort & Spa,
Al Sufouh Road
☎ +971 4 316 5550
rhodestwenty10.com
In my opinion, one of the best dining
experiences in Dubai. Why? What
chefs look for when we dine is choice of
ingredients matched with technique and
simplicity. This is what we earn our money
doing, and believe you me, not all well-
known chefs get it. This chef and his team
does. It may not be the 'hottest' place, the
one on everyone's lips, but it is on mine.

101 Dining Lounge and Bar
West Crescent, The Palm
☎ +971 4 440 1030
thepalm.oneandonlyresorts.com/
cuisine/101.aspx
Great simple decor sitting on a man-made
wonder of the world. One of the better
places to eat at The Palm, an artificial
island in the shape of a palm tree, just
metres off the coast.

Istanbul

I visit mosques and markets,
and meet a man known as the
God of Meat.

Surviving Istanbul airport is a test of your temperament. It makes Denpasar airport look like a meditation retreat. Once you're past this, a magic door opens to a city full of hidden treasures. This city will not hand anything to you on a plate – seek and you will find; be lazy and it will not forgive you. Adventurers only need apply! Also, make sure you pre-book transport to your chosen hotel. Taxis are for Turkish speakers only. The distance from the airport to the city can be quite a journey, mainly due to the traffic. On Sundays it's about half the time as there's less congestion. If you can refrain from pulling your hair out, use the time to sit back and soak up the view of this glorious place of antiquity, tumult, and raw beauty.

I hit the hotel with luggage in hand but there is no time to unpack or freshen up. I have heard of at least a dozen restaurants promising exactly what I'm here to discover. What is that exactly? Freshly baked, wafer-thin crisp flatbread, for a start, topped with wilted parsley and raw nettles. How about globe artichokes cooked in olive oil, resting on a bed of fragrant rice? Or delicately chargrilled anchovy fillets draped over a bed of chopped, deep red tomatoes with a squeeze of lemon juice? Then there is the fresh, wood-oven-baked poppyseed bagel loaded with goats' curd and drizzled with honey, sold from a humble street-corner vendor. Spit-roasted lamb, sliced feather-thin, melded into a soft steamed bun topped with meltingly slow-cooked peppers and tomatoes. Dairy here can be touch and go; for the most part it is pasteurised to buggery, left lifeless and tasteless, but a type of local cheese called *tulum*, a salty feta they mature by wrapping it in goat skin, is so renowned the locals call it the 'king of feta'. Oh and then there is the *lokum* or Turkish delight, only available to those who have inside knowledge of where to find the best. If there is still room, you then move on to baklava filled with clotted cream and the finest pistachios, drenched in honey. ➜

1   The view across the Bay of Bosphorus.
2   Roast corn is sold everywhere from carts like this one – makes a great snack at any time.
3–5 The entrance to a mosque. The taps are so visitors can wash their feet before going in – an important part of the purification ritual.
6–8 Making baklava.

Yes, if you haven't figured it out yet, I'm not here to find restaurants with three-star service and fancy toilets. I'm here to eat. With my food goggles firmly strapped on, I want an education, a history lesson if you will, a journey of discovery. Why is this city, where Asia meets Europe, practically forgotten by the modern international food community when it should be worshipped? I will endeavour to find the answer to this and many other vexing questions, and I have just a few hours to do it.

Unexpectedly, I manage to hook up with Batuhan Piatti. Half-Italian and half-Turkish on his father's side, he now hosts the Turkish version of *Masterchef* as well as a TV program called *Life Is. Beautiful.* He was the former executive chef of the Cipriani hotel chain but called it a day on abnormal kitchen hours in 2010. There is no better authority on how to make the most of my thirty-six hours in this mysterious city.

First stop: Taksim Square. Currently a hotbed of political protests by the young population, it has come to symbolise democratic freedom in Turkey. The tension is everywhere around us; riot police in full gear form long lines and heavy armoured police cars are parked on every corner. With midnight upon us, young people gather in exuberant clusters everywhere. Their body language doesn't betray the slightest sign of aggression or tension, they just seem to be boisterous teens hanging out of the steamed burger joints and kebab bars.

We intend to seek out an excellent place to eat seafood located in Chihangir, a few minutes from Taksim Square. It's renowned for its premium fresh fish. Make your choice and have it grilled to order. But it's getting pretty late for a sit-down meal, so instead we steer a little further into Beyoglu, where lies Istanbul's version of fast food at Sampiyon. They are famous for two dishes: lambs' intestines fried with tomatoes and onions then served in a baguette, and deep-fried mussel skewers. Both are delicious and deeply satisfying. I also find people approaching the busy counter and scooping up steamed mussels stuffed with rice, squeezing a quarter of a lemon on top and devouring them, then dropping a coin on the counter and moving on. Sated, and with the candle well and truly burnt at both ends, we decide to call it a night. ➔

9   The Obelisk of Theodosius, which has been in Istanbul since the fourth century.

10   Dolmabahce Mosque, on the European coast of the Bosphorus.

11   A flag seller at the markets.

12   Deep frying, Turkish style.

My guide, Lino Strangis, Consul General to Turkey, is a man on a mission, however. He sees me as his guest, and with that he is charged with a duty to show me all his fair city has to offer. We have only met hours before, but he drags Cory and me into the diplomatic car. Aussie flags fluttering from the side mirrors, we race through the traffic to our destination: a small group of street stalls in the back streets of Ortakoy, where a veritable feast awaits. My eyes are immediately drawn to what looks like oversized crispy golden tubes of fat sitting over red-hot coals. Beside the grill a cook chops and scrapes away at an already prepared piece, which turns out to be a sheep intestine, harbouring layers of honeycombed tripe. After being cooked slowly for hours over the coals, the golden orb of crisp fat is finely chopped with great theatre and then fried with onions then arranged over ripe tomatoes before chilli and cumin are added for fragrance and kick. A cheap local version of a baguette is fried in the remaining fat, then filled to the brim with this succulent tripe mixture. A few take-away Efes (the local lager), and we are sitting on the Bosphorus waxing lyrical about life in one of the most chaotic cities in the world.

Lino says, 'It is one in the morning and look around you, how many people are here on a Monday night, talking, laughing. Meanwhile back in Australia we are all worried about the next bill, or trying to work out where the best catchment zone is for the school of our choice, or we're behind a computer. We are slowly slipping away from the meaning of life. Life here, for the majority, is about now, not tomorrow. These people are happier.'

I ponder this profound reflection, feeling such a sense of place, as another cargo ship with its lights out hunkers past under the guidance of a half moon. Cory and I shoot an air rifle at a line of balloons at its direction into the Bosphorus, for five lira each. Try doing that back on the Yarra! I am coming to see that Istanbul is a city of self-discovery. I am a better person for it. ➤

13–15 The Egyptian Spice Bazaar in Istanbul, which has been running since the sixteenth century.

The doner kebab

Turkey is the home of the kebab, a staple of Ottoman cuisine right back to the time of the empire. Of course, foodies of Middle Eastern descent will vigorously argue this point, but there is no greater concentration of kebab restaurants and shops anywhere in the world than on the streets of Istanbul. Walking those streets, talking to locals, chefs and devoted foodies, I hear time and again of a ballsy concept called *Gunaydin*. Word is that a local legend by the name of Cuneyt Asan, owner of a chain of kebab shops, doner kebab shops, and butchers under the *Gunaydin* banner, is renowned as the God of Meat. There is even a photo installation featuring him at MONA in Tasmania. 'God of Meat' is some boast, so naturally I have to investigate first-hand. Batuhan agrees to drive me to meet this man at his 'temple', his shop in the upmarket seaside suburb of Bostanci on the Asian side of the Bosphorus.

My first impressions of Cuneyt are that he is a thinker, he is a dreamer, and he could probably land a plane by semaphore the way he wildly gesticulates while shouting passionately in Turkish. Batuhan kindly translates at a volume that doesn't shatter glass. Cunyet tells me the twenty million locals who inhabit this city simply don't buy ready portioned meat, let alone dry-aged meat from a specialist butcher. Most simply look for cheap beef at the market. It has taken him forty years but now he has a band of loyal customers. He generously serves us some of his premium grilled lamb and I am stunned to discover that it has the texture and mouthfeel of waygu beef. This guy is truly one of a kind. His forty shops combined take a total of one million dollars a day! There are no menus in a true Turkish kebab shop, he explains, as Turks are too impatient. They just want to be fed and they will tell you when they have had enough! ➜

16   İstiklal Avenue, one of the most famous streets in Istanbul for food, shopping and nightlife as well as cultural attractions and historic architecture.

17   The little streets in and around İstiklal Avenue are also worth exploring, particularly for food shopping.

My meeting then gets a little weird and wonderful when Cuneyt whips out a few shots of himself dressed in a tuxedo, hugging a dry-aged carcass of beef. I do the polite thing and laugh. This kicks him off and before I know it, he has the television in the middle of the restaurant running, slipping in a DVD showcasing all his television appearances. With remote in hand he yells commentary to Batuhan for him to translate to me. He has basically cut a reel of all his television appearances that cycles over and over again. Absolute classic!

After Cuneyt composes himself with a few deep breaths and pops his Instagram app in his pocket, he gets back to showing me the art of a great kebab. It starts with a deboned leg of Simmental beef, cut into fine slices lengthways, then marinated overnight in a mixture of milk, onion juice, white pepper and salt. It is then skewered very tightly on a steel rod and roasted over hot coals for several hours. ●

18   MADO started as an ice-cream company in 1850 and has since become a popular restaurant chain.
19   Just one of the many varieties of halva that is a specialty of the region.

Dressed anchovies with pide

Serves 4

For the adventurous, 'aspiration' when planning a journey can often lead to 'inspiration' when the journey is concluded, and the food stalls under and around Galatta bridge certainly inspired me. I loved watching small fishing boats backing up to the docks and offloading fresh anchovies (hamsi), which were then grilled over hot coals and placed in bread with tomato and onion. One of my all-time favourite food experiences. This dish is all about freshness, so make sure you ask your local fish supplier for the freshest anchovies – they might even clean them for you. If fresh anchovies are not available, use baby mackerel, red mullet or even whitebait instead.

12 fresh anchovies
1 large red onion, finely diced
2 cloves garlic, crushed
1 chilli, thinly sliced
¼ cup (60 ml) extra virgin olive oil
sea salt
2–3 tablespoons oregano leaves
2 lemons, cut in half
¼ cup (50 g) baby capers, rinsed and drained
2–2½ tablespoons apple vinegar
8 pieces pide or a flatbread
small basil leaves, to garnish

To clean the anchovies, make a incision down the belly of each fish to the tail, flip the fish over to its upright position (swimming position) then gently push down on the fish to butterfly it. Turn it over and pull the head away from the fillets – this will also remove the main vertebrae so you are left with butterflied fish fillets.

Combine the onion, garlic and chilli. Set aside.

Heat 1 tablespoon olive oil in a non-stick frying pan over an induction set on 7 or a gas burner over medium–high heat. Season the anchovies with salt then add them to the pan, skin-side down, and cook until the skin is crispy. Flip them over and cook for a further 2 minutes or until the fish are cooked through. Add the oregano and a squeeze of lemon juice, then remove the fish from the pan. Arrange them neatly on a tray or serving platter, skin-side up, and rest in a warming drawer.

Heat 1 tablespoon olive oil in the same frying pan and cook the onion, garlic and chilli over medium–high heat for 2 minutes. Add the capers and apple vinegar, then check the seasoning and remove from the heat. Spoon the dressing over the anchovies and leave to marinate for a few minutes.

Return the pan to medium heat, add the remaining olive oil and a good pinch of salt, then cook the pide or flatbread for 1 minute on 1 side only. Remove.

Scatter the basil over the fish. Serve with the bread on the side (or for something a little different, serve the anchovies in a newspaper cone).

Meat and potatoes
the Turkish way

Serves 4

Lamb in this part of the world is excellent, though
I would say it is closer to hogget than lamb. The smell
of charcoal and barbecues attracts the people to
the streets like pigeons to a park bench covered in
crumbs. Those with an adventurous palate try
a classic dish called Kokorec, which contains lamb
sweetbreads wrapped in lamb intestines grilled over
charcoal with plenty of salt, fresh tomatoes and
a hint of chilli. This recipe contains pickled lamb's
tongue, which you will probably need to order in
advance from your butcher.

**800 g lamb loin with fat still attached,
cut into 25 g slices**
sea salt
**4 large potatoes, peeled and thinly sliced,
then cut into matchsticks**
1 litre water
**good handful of flat-leaf parsley,
finely chopped**
½ cup (125 ml) extra virgin olive oil
**2 brown onions, cut in half, peeled
and
thinly sliced**
2 cloves garlic, roughly chopped
**4 smoked pickled lamb's tongues, peeled
and thinly sliced**
1 long red chilli, seeded and finely chopped
2 tablespoons apple vinegar
handful of oregano, finely chopped
rocket salad, to serve (optional)

Preheat a chargrill or barbecue to medium–high.

Season the lamb slices with salt, then cook
over hot coals for 1 minute on each side. Transfer
to a serving platter and rest in the warming drawer
at 35°C.

Arrange the potato matchsticks in a single
layer in the base of a wide-based saucepan, add the
water and parsley and season well with salt. Bring
to the boil, then remove the pan from the heat and
set aside to cool – you still want the potato to have
a little crunch.

Heat a frying pan over an induction set on 9 or
a gas burner over high heat, drizzle 3–4 tablespoons
olive oil into the pan and fry the onion and garlic
for 3–4 minutes or until caramelised. Drain the
potato and add to the pan, then fry until tender.
Add the lamb's tongue, chilli and vinegar and warm
through. Check the seasoning and drizzle with the
remaining olive oil.

To serve, arrange the lamb slices on a platter,
then top each with a small pile of the potato
mixture and a scattering of oregano. If possible,
serve with a beautiful seasonal rocket salad on
the side.

Baklava

Serves 4

Surprisingly, Gunaydin is also Butauhan's favourite stop for baklava. Cuneyt Asan found it frustrating that he could not find consistent baklava in his favourite tea and coffee houses so he decided to open a kitchen dedicated to this Turkish classic. After witnessing first hand how much work goes into rolling the dough into layers so thin they will dry to a thin crisp in seconds, I couldn't help comparing the coordination required of the pastry cook with that of a professional dancer. I mentioned this to Cuneyt and his humble response was really quite profound: 'We know a lot of things in this country but we have trouble explaining ourselves.'

To make this dessert at home I suggest using filo pasty instead of attempting to make the very difficult traditional dough. True baklava purists agree there are only 3 ingredients that really matter when you are making the best: the butter, the pistachios and the person making it.

10 sheets filo pastry
1 litre ghee (made from spring sheep's milk)
or clarified butter
200 g shelled antep (Turkish) pistachios,
roughly chopped
500 g clotted cream
finely grated zest of 1 lemon
100 g honey
100 ml water

Preheat the oven on the conventional setting to 190°C. Have a 20 cm square baking tin ready.

Unravel the filo pastry and lay it out to form a square that is 3 times the size of your baking tin. Brush each layer of pastry with ghee then sprinkle with a good layer of pistachios – you want the pistachios to cover an area just slightly larger than your baking tin. Randomly scatter the clotted cream over the pistachios, followed by the lemon zest. Continue layering until you have used all the filo, reserving some of the cream and pistachios for the garnish.

Fold the sides of the pastry over the top, encasing the filling, and place in the baking tin. Brush the top with ghee and, if you like, mark it into diamond or other shapes; otherwise just leave it plain. Bake for about 10 minutes or until golden.

While the pastry is in the oven heat the honey and water together in a small saucepan until boiling. When the pastry is nice and golden take it out of the oven and ladle the hot honey water over the top (be careful it may splatter). Leave to rest for 10 minutes, then spoon over the reserved cream and sprinkle with the remaining pistachios. Cut into pieces and enjoy while it's still hot.

Visitor tips

Hotels

The House Hotel Bosphorus
Salhane Sokak No.1, Ortaköy 34347
☎ +90 212 327 77 87
thehousehotel.com
Ever been woken up by a trainee imam at four in the morning, intoning the call to prayer on a loudspeaker? I have, and let me tell you it is certainly one way to know you are in Istanbul! It was as if this bloke was sitting right outside my window.

The House is in the best location in all of Istanbul. Right on the Bosphorus river; I mean literally on it. I book a deluxe Bosphorus suite for 370€ a night, not an insignificant amount of money but a worthy investment. There's a small sitting room with a TV, and it's all very white and fresh with simple decor leading to a very small bedroom with a comfy bed. The bathroom is not big enough to swing a kitten in, let alone a cat. That aside, the terrace on the first level where breakfast is served is without a doubt the best place in Turkey to be on a glorious sunny morning. This alone would make me stay here, just with earplugs next time.

The Four Seasons Bosphorus
Yıldız Mh., Çırağan Cd No: 28, Beşiktaş
☎ +90 212 381 4000
fourseasons.com/Istanbul-Bosphorus
The larger, more popular and energetic of the two properties. The location is just jaw-dropping; the main building backs directly on to the majestic Bosphorus river. Its architecture is considerably earlier, and the layout features a very limited number of rooms and suites. When booking you need to insist that your room has a Bosphorus view. I was lucky enough to be staying in a suite with an outside deck, nearly as large as the room itself, which had a magnificent, unspoilt view of the river and passing container ships. They look so dramatic and have a such a sense of importance as they power downstream out to the open ocean.

Service here is first-class; when we buy a 250-gram tin of caviar from the markets and request some garnish from room service. Within fifteen minutes, and at no charge, we are delivered a trolley bearing the *piece de la resistance* of caviar garnishes: petite blinis, chopped egg, finely diced shallots and creme fraiche, along with a clutch of cheeses and crackers, champagne and crystal flutes, and a bowl of fragrant strawberries.

The Four Seasons Sultanahmet
Tevkifhane caddesi No. 1 , Sultanahmet-Eminönü, 34110
☎ +90 212 402 3000
fourseasons.com/IstanbulSultanahmet
This was the stay of a lifetime. Four Seasons Hotels are the benchmark for me in world-class five-star hotels. Sultanahmet is a tourist magnet, as the blue mosque up the hill is a major drawcard. I was starstruck to discover that before it was a five-star hotel, it was the infamous prison the film *Midnight Express* was based on. The rooms are not cheap but they are undeniably luxurious. The main restaurant also serves great Turkish-inspired dishes from a buffet. It's the simple things done exceptionally well that give it the edge, and it has an understated class that just makes me feel privileged to be here. The early-morning call for prayer announcing the dawn gives you a sense of place. Back this up with service that is second to none and this hotel deserves your attention.

Restaurants

Kantin Restaurant
Teşvikiye Mh., Akkavak Sk No:30, 34365
☎ +90 212 219 3114
kantin.biz
The home of simply great home-cooked seasonal Turkish food made with passion. The blackboard tells you the specials of the day. Salads are displayed on a counter. Hot dishes include *hamsi*, which is grilled anchovies with lemon, parsley and sea salt, or the smokiest, most delicate kofta you will ever taste. They call the chef here the Stephanie Alexander of Turkey.

Wet burgers

Galata Bridge
Hobyar Eminönü Mh., Hoca Kasım Köprüsü Sk, Fatih
☎ +90 212 243 9501
and
Kizilkayalar's Wet Burgers
Sira Selviler Cad. No:2/L, Taksim MeydanI Istiklal Girisi
kizilkayalar.com.tr
and
Taksim Square
istanbul-ulasim.com.tr
Who would think that a pile of burgers ten high and fifty deep sitting in what looks like a mini hammam would actually taste so bloody good. 'Wet burgers' contain only tomato, beef fat and a shrunken patty encased inside a steamed bun. There are two places that boast the best versions: under the Galata Bridge and just off Taksim Square. Locals say Kizilkayalar is the best. Apparently, nowhere else in the world do these burgers exist, and they simply cannot be missed.

London

Where black cabs rule,
and we discover that pub food
has come a long way.

What is it about London that no other city has? What makes the old girl tick? One answer surfaces time and again: class, class and class. Her Majesty's homeland is the only place in the world where I feel compelled to look for the nearest handkerchief retailer. I'm overcome with the urge to pop a natty square of cotton in the left-hand pocket of my suit jacket.

Another of London's unique cultural assets is its black cab drivers. These men and women are an institution. Tell them an address or the name of a cafe and they know it! And more importantly, you feel safe.

In my lowly opinion, London has grown up. Its middle class is well defined and now shapes this city. Design, food and fashion have transformed the once crime-ridden and poverty-stricken back streets; coffee roasters sit next to cheese shops. Rooftop gardens now overflow with strawberry plants.

I can now tell you what London food is in a few words: warm, earthy and proper. Fish and chips is not just fish and chips any more. It is smoked haddock, line-caught off the west coast of Wales in a crisp beer batter, and chips hand-cut from new-season jersey royals, cooked twice in biodynamic beef fat. You want shellfish? It's brought down on the overnight train, live, from Scotland. Pubs now serve locally brewed beer. They are still places to spend the afternoon or evening in but they boast some of the best food in all of Europe. ➜

1–3   London is a huge city; starting at the middle and moving out is as good an approach as any when you've got one day to fit it all in. We ticked off a few essentials: Nelson's Column and Trafalgar Square, cheesy postcards, a black cab and a red double-decker bus.

4   Michael Jeanes, Patricia Jeanes and writer Scott Murray in a black cab; these vehicles are truly among London's unique cultural assets.

5   Borough Market, one of London's most famous food markets. The farmers' market concept has really taken off all over England and they are now popping up all over the place.

Coffee in London

It is a stunning, sunny Saturday morning in East London. 'Coffee' around these parts has traditionally been a swear word. Happily, though, you can now expect great-quality coffee. Gone are the days that no one complained at over-roasted, over-extracted, bitter coffee.

James Hoffmann is a former world barista champion who owns a coffee roasting company called Square Mile. He is part of the revolutionising of the cafe scene. The espresso I have just inhaled was aromatic, delicate, spicy with a delicious-looking crema, perfectly balanced with a touch of acidity contrasting with a hint of sweetness. Bon voyage, jet lag!

The north-east festival

The north-east festival is a curious beast, a mix of food, culture and music, located in the middle of nowhere. We couldn't get through the crowds in time so Chris Bonello, executive chef of Bistro Vue, had to do the cooking demonstration I'd been booked to do.

We arrive as the demo gets underway, the marquee is packed with a good few hundred people. I hear the MC announce Chris as Shannon Bennett, owner of the iconic Vue de Monde. Chris has no idea what to say so just starts waving and smiling bravely. ●

6–8   James from Square Mile coffee, with his roasting and grinding machines.

9   Fresh seafood at the markets.

10   The Scottish Blackface lamb, a heritage breed which is having a resurgence in Britain's new food scene.

11   The lamb, now in the form of tasty burgers being grilled for our lunch.

12   Arriving at the festival.

13   We take a breather before the cooking demonstration.

14   The festival, where we somehow get roped into wearing lightbulbs on our heads.

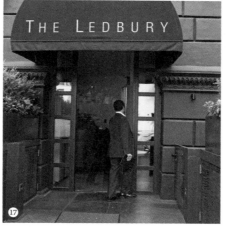

15–18 Pub food in England has come a long way from the choice between the obligatory packet of cheese 'n' onion crisps or pork scratchings that used to be on offer. We ate everything from pan-roasted mackerel to king crab salad in these pubs, washed down with a pint of real ale.

19 With Brett Graham, owner of the Michelin-starred Harwood Arms.

20 The famous circular entrance to All Souls Church in London.

Bubble and squeak

Serves 4

There are recorded recipes for bubble and squeak dating back to around 1830, when thinly sliced salted beef and chopped cabbage were fried together as a simple meal. The name comes from the noise it makes in the pan as it cooks. A little tip: don't replace the duck fat with vegetable oil as you won't be able to achieve the high temperatures that give you the bubbles and the squeaks, plus the crust won't be quite as burnt and satisfying. The New Generation 6000 drying function gives this dish a very restaurant feel with crispy kale. To be honest, this recipe would fit well at home and on any good cafe/brasserie menu.

50 g trimmed kale leaves, well washed
sea salt
vegetable oil, for sprinkling
200 g smoked haddock
2 medium potatoes, peeled and washed
50 g butter
1 cup (80 g) shredded white cabbage
½ brown onion, peeled and thinly sliced
¾ cup (75 g) finely chopped cauliflower
100 g duck fat
4 eggs
½ cup (15 g) picked watercress, well washed

To make the kale dehydrated and crispy, go to special oven functions/drying/85°C/2 hours. Arrange the kale leaves on a rack, season with salt and sprinkle with vegetable oil, then place in the oven for 2 hours.

About 40 minutes before you want to eat, cook the haddock for 5 minutes in a steamer at 100% steam. Remove to a plate.

Season the potatoes with salt, then cook in the steamer for 20 minutes – make sure the potatoes are still a touch undercooked so they can be grated. Remove and set aside to cool slightly, then grate with a coarse cheese grater.

Melt the butter in a frying pan over high heat and lightly saute the cabbage, onion and cauliflower. Set aside to cool.

Flake the haddock into a mixing bowl, then add the potato and cabbage mixture. Season lightly if needed (remember the smoked haddock is salted already) and mix well. Shape the mixture into 8 patties and press each into an 8 cm ring mould.

Melt half the duck fat in a non-stick frying pan, with the induction set on 6. Place the patties in the pan and cook for 3–4 minutes or until lightly browned on each side.

Meanwhile, melt the remaining duck fat in a non-stick frying pan, with the induction set on 4, and gently fry the eggs, taking care not to overcook the yolks.

Place 2 patties on each plate, then top one of them with a fried egg. Arrange watercress on the side and scatter the crispy kale around the plate.

Duck meatloaf with beetroot slaw

Serves 8

Hands up if meatloaf is at the absolute bottom of your list of favourite recipes? It is for me. (I won't mention that my wife used to put evaporated milk in her 'heirloom' recipe.) Anyway, I think it deserves a reinvention, and this little duck number does just that. I have replaced the cheap broiled mince with top-quality duck meat, the fat in the small portion of pork mince adds moisture, and I've thrown in a few other little flavourings. I think this dish can be a real winner for the family table.

**2 duck breasts, fat removed (keep aside)
    and meat minced**
2½ tablespoons water
1 onion, cut in half, peeled and finely chopped
**4 duck legs, deboned and minced
    (or 750 g duck mince)**
250 g pork mince
4 eggs, lightly beaten
**1 carrot, finely grated (preferably with
    a microplane)**
2 tablespoons chopped flat-leaf parsley
1 tablespoon thyme leaves
1 tablespoon English mustard, or to taste
2 cups (140) g coarse fresh breadcrumbs
sea salt
mustard leaves, to serve

Beetroot slaw
1 large beetroot
**1 small onion, cut in half, peeled
    and cut into thin strips**
1 tablespoon mayonnaise
sea salt

Place the duck fat removed from the breast in a small saucepan with the water and melt over medium heat. Pass through a fine-mesh sieve into a small frying pan and heat over medium heat. Add the onion and saute until softened but not coloured. Set aside.

Place the duck meat and pork mince in a mixing bowl, add the beaten egg and mix together well with your hands or a large mixing spoon. Add the onion, carrot, parsley, thyme, mustard, breadcrumbs and salt and combine well. Transfer to a 25 cm × 8 cm × 7 cm loaf tin or terrine dish and smooth the top, then place in the oven.

Go to oven functions/moisture plus/140°C/automatic 3 bursts of steam/20 minutes/place cup to draw water/start. This will automatically cook the meatloaf for 1 hour. When it's ready, take it out and let it cool at room temperature, then rest it in the fridge overnight. You could also serve it warm, if preferred.

To make the beetroot slaw, wash and peel the beetroot, then cut it lengthways into 2 mm thick slices (a mandolin is great for this, if you have one). Using a sharp knife, cut the sliced beetroot into thin strips. Combine the beetroot, onion and mayonnaise in a bowl, then season to taste with salt. Cover and store in the fridge until you are ready to serve.

Turn out meatloaf onto a board and cut into thick slices. Serve with mustard leaves and beetroot slaw.

Spotted dick with whipped custard

Serves 4

The history of spotted dick is fascinating and rather mysterious. Some people attribute it to Dick Turpin, a highwayman in Northern England, who became the stuff of legend after his execution in 1739 for deer poaching. Canny parents would get their children, who regarded Dick Turpin as a hero, to eat dried fruit by placing it in suet pudding and calling it spotted dick after Turpin, saying it was his favourite pud.

Word has it that if you cook the pudding in a rounded mould you have a better chance of evenly distributing the currants through the batter than if you use a baking tray. Personally, I don't mind so I'm using a tray here, but I mention it for those who do. I have added whipped custard to the dish by placing it in a cream whip gun. Fewer calories that way! But of course it's fine to serve it with regular custard if preferred.

On the day of recipe testing at the Miele Gallery on Cavendish Place, something extraordinary happened. 73-year-old Mr Manning walked into the gallery, escorted by his lovely wife, and it turns out Mr Manning eats spotted dick every day. Literally! He goes to incredible lengths to keep this habit alive, stocking up with a year's supply from Waitrose (they only sell spotted dick in the winter months so he has a dedicated deep freezer in the garage to cope with his wonderful addiction). Mrs Manning detests the smell of spotted dick so Mr Manning installed a Miele microwave in the garage and a kettle, so he can sit in comfortable solitude every day with his pudding and cup of tea, contemplating the world and its tribulations. What, I ask you, could be better in life?!

480 g butter, softened
560 g caster sugar
12 large eggs, lightly beaten
finely grated zest of 2 large oranges
1½ cups (240 g) currants
2 cups (300 g) self-raising flour, sifted
90 ml milk
icing sugar, for dusting

Whipped custard
2 cups (500 ml) milk
35 g custard powder
45 g caster sugar
¼ cup (60 ml) milk, extra

Lightly butter a steaming tray or deep baking tray that has a tight-fitting lid (use several layers of foil if you don't have a lid).

Cream the butter and sugar together in an electric mixer until soft. Gradually add the beaten egg, a little at a time, making sure each addition is incorporated before adding more. Add the orange zest, currants, flour and milk and fold in gently.

Spoon the batter into the prepared tray. Cover tightly with foil, then place the lid on top (or extra layers of foil) and press down to get a tight seal.

Preheat the steamer to 100% steam and cook for 1 hour.

Meanwhile, to make the whipped custard, heat the milk in a heavy-based saucepan over an induction set on 5. You want it to come to just below the boil. Blend together the custard powder, sugar and extra milk in a small bowl. When the milk comes to the boil, whisk one quarter of it into the custard mixture, then return it all to the pan. Bring it to the boil, whisking constantly, then immediately transfer it to a cream whip gun and place the lid on. Charge with 2 gas bulbs and shake well.

At the end of the cooking time remove the foil and insert a skewer into the sponge; if it comes out clean it is ready.

Spoon the spotted dick onto plates and serve with the whipped custard from the cream gun. Dust with icing sugar to finish.

Visitor tips

Hotels

Claridges Hotel
49 Brook St, W1K 4HR
☎ +44 20 7629 8860
claridges.co.uk
Even the cab driver is excited that
I'm staying at Claridges. For me, it sits
atop a pedestal shared with very few others.
Re-touched but never reinvented. A great
hotel should be an extension of one's home:
their living room is your living room.
The answer is always yes, never no.

The Dorchester Hotel
Park Lane, Mayfair, W1K 1QA
☎ +44 20 7317 6530
thedorchester.com
This hotel is where Elizabeth Taylor
requested a room with a large bathtub;
no problem, they installed it for her!
Everybody who checked in was Elizabeth
Taylor. My room is classic Dorchester:
luxurious country chic.
    The hotel houses some great dining
rooms, and the lobby and lounge are
visually luxurious. It feels as if I have
wandered into an era where champagne
flowed like water, men changed their suits
twice a day and women were mesmerising.
The best of London doesn't have to show
off nor does she have anything to prove,
particularly when you take the time to slow
down and notice what she has to offer; this
city is a piece of work with a lot of power
and might.

Hazlitt's Hotel →
6 Frith Street, Soho Square, W1D 3JA
☎ +44 20 7434 1771
hazlittshotel.com
Two Georgian houses joined together
to make one of the most characterful
hotels I've ever stayed in. Each super-
comfortable room is filled with antiques;
it's like stepping back in time, right in the
middle of the hippest part of London.

Pubs

The Harwood Arms
Walham Grove, Fulham SW6 1QP
☎ +44 20 7386 1847
harwoodarms.com
The only London pub with a Michelin star.
Wild hare, Scotch eggs, fresh sourdough,
grilled mackerel and pickled onions with
locally brewed ales and modern pilsners.
A young crowd with the foodie buzz, all
wanting to know where the hare was shot.

Newman Street Tavern ↓
48 Newman St, W1T 1QQ
☎ +44 20 3667 1445
The Newman Street Tavern, open from
10:30 a.m. for brunch, bar snacks, lunch,
all-day dining and dinner. Locals use this
place as a bit of everything. London pub
food at its best and simplest.

Restaurants

Brasserie Chavot
41 Conduit Street, Mayfair
☎ +44 20 7183 6425
brasseriechavot.com
Eric Chavot's menu is as Parisian as
a French poodle sipping Evian. Beef tartare
is generous, with half a poulet eggshell
resting on top of a moulded mound of
flavoured beef mince. A parfait of chicken
livers is better than good.

Restaurant Story
201 Tooley St, SE1 2UE
☎ +44 20 7183 2117
restaurantstory.co.uk
Intimate, and the main service kitchen is
glassed in so you can observe all the action.
The wine list is small but has something for
everyone, and the snacks come out in quirky,
unexpected forms such as radishes stuffed
with pate. It is a great start, and impressive
dishes follow. This guy can cook! In some
dishes you really taste London, such as in
the beef dripping candle with a traditional
candle holder at the base, seasoned with
salt that catches the dripping fat, served
with bread. Such theatre.

Plane Food by Gordon Ramsay
Terminal 5, Heathrow, TW6 2GA
☎ +44 20 8897 4545
gordonramsay.com/planefood
Plane picnics for £12 – three packaged
courses from a choice of four entrees,
four mains and four desserts.

Tamarind Restaurant
20 Queen St, W1J 5PR
☎ +44 20 7629 3561
tamarindrestaurant.com
Prices are generally very reasonable:
around £15–25 for a main dish. You only
need two between three with some rice,
breads and a vegetable side and you will be
completely satisfied, mind, body and soul.

Mexico City

Where insects are surprisingly
delicious, chocolate is good in savoury
dishes, and we visit a creepy island.

Mexico City right now is the hottest place on the planet for food and excitement. There are no rules other than: have fun and have your wits about you. It is not for the faint-hearted but for the brave, the rewards are priceless.

Let me tell you, smuggling kangaroo meat into Mexico City isn't easy. It wasn't *really* smuggling; I declared it on the sheet. Customs were interested in my story, and why the hell I wanted to bring the meat into a city boasting more incredible ingredients than I could poke a stick at, but it just was not to be. I was encouraged, though, by the fact that the customs agents were incredibly friendly and humble. They made Australian Customs look like the Ringwraiths guarding Mordor.

The airport is reasonably close to the posh downtown area of Polanco. Originally the Jewish quarter of Mexico City, it has all the trimmings of a first-world city-within-a-city. Manicured gardens, fancy shops and major hotels such as the Hyatt and the W. I check in to a small place the Miele team and our guest chef for the trip, Martha Brockmann, have chosen, Las Alcobas. The hotel is a perfect fit with its neighbourhood: modern and intimate, with an air of everyday luxury.

Sam Leizorek, the owner, greets me and gives me a tour. He is particularly proud of the hotel restaurant, run by American chef Justin Ermini with his Mexican wife managing the front of house. The restaurant has a great feel, with understated modern decor that really reflects how stylish this city can be when it turns it on.

I'm dragged away kicking and screaming. I have so many questions to ask Sam but it is 4 p.m. and the local team are hungry. It's the weekend, when the locals eat lunch late, and they don't hold back. These weekend lunches, whether in the home or at a restaurant, surrounded by friends and family, are a veritable feast. I am taken to La Roma and La Condesa, two adjacent precincts of Mexico City that host a wide variety of places to eat. ➜

1 Mexico City's Metropolitan Cathedral, built by the Spanish over several centuries from the sixteenth century onwards.
2 A stunning example of Spanish Colonial Revival architecture.
3 Markets in Mexico are the best place to buy traditional crafts and textiles.

The area attracts a lot of young diners. The decor is simple, unremarkable if anything, but it is where local culture meets great food. Eugenia, my host, is adamant that when it comes to authentic Mexican food, the chef of La Condesa, chef and food historian Ricardo Muñoz Zurita, literally wrote the book. Literally. Entitled *Diccionario Enciclopedico de Gastronomia Mexicana*, it is *the* encyclopaedia of Mexican food, and it does not disappoint. The latest worldwide food trend is for chefs to serve insects as the funky new super food. Personally, if the cuisine is not Thai, Chinese or Mexican then I think this trend is a load of rubbish. Back at La Roma, I put out of my mind the fact that I am about to nosh on creepy crawlies usually seasoned with a squirt of Mortein back home, and order a spread. The bugs are served in different ways. White, larvae-type worms are roasted and wrapped in a taco with guacamole and pickled red onions. They taste of reduced chicken stock and are texturally very pleasing. I hope to paint Mexican cuisine in a great light as the food here is simply outstanding, with or without grasshoppers.

I notice new groups of people arriving; it takes them at least five minutes to get to their tables as they give full rounds of kisses and waves to each table. It is now 5 p.m. and we are still in the middle of lunch!

We walk out the door at 6 p.m. with two hours to go until dinner. My inner health nut demands that I pull on the jogging shoes and hit the pavement, and I obey. The great thing about being in Polanco is everything is at walking distance. The streets are completely safe. Minutes from the hotel is the largest park in Mexico, the Bosque de Chapultepec, and jogging through it, it's easy to forget you are in such a large city. The zoo, museum and gallery are all in this park, along with many street performers and food stands. Twelve kilometres and an hour later, I am ready for dinner. ➜

4–6   At Casa Crespo, where Oscar Carrizosa was the guest chef.
7–11   A few different ways to serve bugs.

Dinner at Quintonil probably saves me a week of research and a month of footwork. Here, the gastronomic inventions dreamt up by its head chef clearly express the flavours and direction of modern Mexican cooking. Quintonil emerged from a partnership between young Mexican chef Jorge Vallejo, widely celebrated for his work and solid career path, and veteran restaurateur Alejandra Flores.

I rise early the next morning and head to the Coyoacan Market, where exotic meats such as lion meat are advertised – along with kangaroo. However, when we asked to see the meat we were told 'No'. I certainly observed armadillo meat being prepared.

If breakfast is at the forefront of your mind then El Cardenal has to be the place. Old-world decor and atmosphere in the heart of the old town. Bookings are not required; there may be a five-minute wait for a table but the vast menu of burritos, egg dishes and tortillas is well worth the journey. Dishes like *conchas con nata,* a crisp breakfast pastry with a soft, sweet filling, and especially the fragrant hot chocolate are a must. Anything you order will be 100 per cent Mexico! Be sure to visit the awe-inspiring city square Zocálo and Centro Historico – the largest city square I have ever walked in.

Then we head to the famed Aztec-built canals of Xochimilco, one hour's drive south of the city, arriving to an array of colour, noise and smells from the street food stalls and bars sitting on the edge of the canal. A UNESCO world heritage site, the area is made up of a network of canals and artificial islands. This area is used for agriculture, where garden beds are made by dredging sediment and silt from the canals. These are called *chinampas;* they were invented by the pre-Hispanic peoples of the region around 1500 years ago as a way to utilise the water and fertile silt of the canals. Originally the shallow waters of two lakes, the canals are now used as mini-highways by farmers and tourists alike to peacefully meander through the lush mix of sporting fields and market gardens. ➔

12　A Mexican organ grinder or *organillero;* these have been an integral part of the city since the end of the nineteenth century.

13　Street stall food – a common sight in Mexico City.

The main mode of transport is a *trajinara*, a colourful gondola-type raft that is propelled by pushing a large pole into the beds at the sides of the canals. We reach several small farms and buy enough produce for the dinner – herbs like lupins, fat hen and wild rocket are in abundance along with many varieties of vegetables. Our last stop is the spookiest of my entire world tour. Being close to the 1st of November and the festival of the dead, the hairs on my skin are already a little attentive, so when we reach a small shrine with a bar and restaurant, festooned with decaying dolls hung from every tree and post within 100 square metres of the landing, I feel quite on edge. The story behind these dolls is intriguing and freaky. It turns out that a local man was witness to a girl drowning at the site. He was haunted by the event and to ward away her spirit, he collected dolls and placed them all over the site. The story goes that in his late seventies, the man had a heart attack and drowned in the exact same spot as the girl, forty-two years later to the day!

The dinner that night was a huge success, with Miele co-owner Dr Reinhard Zinkann flying in to be with us. I get the feeling he is going to miss these trips; we have a great laugh. The next morning we give ourselves three hours to get to the airport. I am amazed to see Reinhard bright as a button in the foyer of the hotel the next morning at 7 a.m., as if he has just had twelve hours' sleep. Maybe I am old before my time!

Mexico City has done it for me. I am hooked. This city has no rival for excitement, people and food. I will be back. ●

14   The doll shrine at the Island of the Dolls –
     one of the creepiest places you'll ever visit.

Grilled corn

Serves 4

This dish was inspired by Mexican street food, and my challenge now is to convince my 4 children that this is the new fast food. If only I could persuade the street vendors to give away a plastic toy with each corn cob, I think I could win them over (minus the chilli!). Cojita is a hard cow's milk cheese that originated in Mexico. If you can't find it, use another hard salty cheese such as parmesan.

4 large corn cobs, peeled (husks reserved)
2 tablespoons grapeseed oil
sea salt
4 spring onions, sliced
1 large jalapeno chilli, seeded and thinly sliced
1 tablespoon roughly chopped coriander
⅓ cup (100 g) Japanese mayonnaise
100 g cotija cheese
lime halves or quarters, to serve
1 teaspoon chilli powder (optional)

Coriander and jalapeno sauce
1 handful of coriander
1 jalapeno chilli
juice of 2 limes
sea salt

Preheat the steamer to 100°C.

Soak the corn husks in water and set aside. Place the corn cobs in the steamer for 15 minutes or until tender.

Remove the corn from the steamer and preheat the oven on grill to 260°C.

Brush the corn with grapeseed oil and season with salt. Lay the soaked husks flat on a baking tray, put the corn on top and place on the top shelf under the grill. Cook, turning, for about 10 minutes or until the corn is coloured and the husk is smoking. The smoke flavour will permeate the corn.

Meanwhile, combine the spring onion, chilli and coriander in a small bowl.

To make the coriander and jalapeno sauce, place the coriander, chilli, lime juice and a pinch of salt in a food processor and blitz until smooth.

Place the corn on a serving platter, then generously spread with the mayonnaise and sprinkle with the spring onion mixture. Grate the cheese over the top, then finish with a good squeeze of lime juice, a little more salt and a dash of chilli powder (if using). Serve hot with the sauce.

Cochinita pibil

Serves 8

This dish is Mexico City's version of pulled pork and is often enjoyed as part of a simple banquet. It is without a doubt my favourite thing to eat here. My friend Martha Brockmann helped me write and test this recipe. I've used traditional pork, but you could try other meats if preferred – just adjust the cooking time accordingly.

220 g achiote paste
400 ml freshly squeezed orange juice
200 ml freshly squeezed lime juice
2 teaspoons dried Mexican oregano
⅓ cup (80 ml) white vinegar
sea salt
1 teaspoon freshly ground black pepper
1.5 kg pork shoulder, cut into large pieces
500 g banana leaves
12–16 regular or black tortillas
4 cups (880 g) cooked brown rice, hot
lemon or lime wedges, to serve

Pickled red onion
2 large red onions, peeled, cut in half
** and thinly sliced**
½ cup (125 ml) white vinegar
1 teaspoon dried Mexican oregano
1 teaspoon sea salt
1 teaspoon freshly ground black pepper

Fried black beans
1 cup (200 g) dried Mexican black beans
1.25 litres water
1 tablespoon pork fat
juice of 1 lime
sea salt

Salsa roja
3 green tomatoes, roughly chopped
3 cloves garlic, crushed
1 white onion, peeled, cut in half and
** very finely minced**
2 jalapeno chillies, seeded and finely chopped
4 tablespoons pickled red onion
sea salt
freshly squeezed lime juice, to taste

Guacamole
2 ripe avocados, peeled and stones removed
1 red onion, peeled, cut in half and finely chopped
handful of coriander, roughly chopped
freshly squeezed lime juice, to taste
sea salt

Place the achiote paste, orange juice, lime juice, oregano, vinegar, salt and pepper in a blender and process until smooth. Scrape the paste into a stainless steel bowl, add the pork and mix until the pork is well coated. Cover and marinate overnight in the fridge.

Meanwhile, to prepare the pickled red onion, combine all the ingredients in a bowl, then spoon into 1 large jar or 2 small jars and refrigerate for 12 hours before using. You won't need it all for this recipe, but leftovers will keep in the fridge for up to 3 weeks.

Preheat the oven on the conventional setting to 160°C.

Line the inside of a large casserole dish with half the banana leaves, then add the pork and cover with the remaining banana leaves. Cover with a lid, then seal the lid with foil and bake for 2 hours or until the meat falls apart when touched. Remove from the oven and leave to rest with the lid on.

While the pork is cooking make a start on the fried black beans. Soak the black beans in 1 litre water for 1 hour. Drain. Place the beans and remaining water in a heavy-based saucepan and cook over medium heat for at least 30 minutes or until soft. Drain, reserving the cooking water. Heat a heavy-based frying pan over an induction set on 6 or a gas burner over medium heat, add the pork fat and beans and cook gently until the beans change colour and develop a slight crust. Stir in 1 tablespoon of the reserved cooking water, then remove from the heat and season to taste with lime juice and salt. Stir well. The beans will be pretty much mashed by now but do not be concerned – this is the objective.

To make the salsa roja, combine the tomato, garlic, onion, chilli and pickled red onion in a food processor and blend until roughly minced. Season to taste with salt and lime juice, then spoon into a small serving bowl or sauce boat.

For the guacamole, place the avocado, onion and coriander in a bowl and mix and mash with a wooden spoon until well combined. Season to taste with lime juice and salt, then spoon into a serving bowl and store in the fridge until needed.

Just before serving, increase the oven temperature to 180°C. Warm the tortillas in the oven for 2 minutes or so.

Serve the pork with the tortillas, rice, fried black beans, salsa, pickled red onion, guacamole and lemon or lime wedges.

Chocolate flan

Serves 8

The cocoa plant is native to Mexico, and has been harvested for food and medicinal purposes for over 5000 years. Chocolate is not always associated with Mexico City but it actually plays an important role in people's diets here. You'll find it in a large array of recipes, from savoury dishes and hot drinks all the way to this very popular chocolate torte. Dulce de leche is essentially a thick milk caramel and it's the super sauce in Mexico, served with everything from crepes to warmed fresh fruit and ice-cream. If you are lucky enough to live in Mexico, it is available already made in a can.

1 × 395 g can sweetened condensed milk
milk, to thin the caramel (optional)
shaved chocolate curls and chocolate crumbs,
**   to garnish (see Note)**

Chocolate flan
400 g caster sugar
2 cups (500 ml) water
1 cup (250 ml) milk
2 cups (500 ml) cream
1 teaspoon ground cinnamon
240 g best-quality dark chocolate buttons,
**   such as Valrhona Guanaja**
5 eggs, lightly beaten
1 egg yolk, lightly beaten
125 g raw sugar

Start by converting the sweetened condensed milk into a caramel. Place the can of condensed milk in a saucepan of water over an induction set on 4 or a gas burner over very low heat and simmer for 3–4 hours. Check the water level regularly and make sure the can is always fully submerged. Take the can out of the pan and cool in iced water for about 20 minutes, then carefully cut it open using a tin opener. Pour the caramel into a sauce boat, ready to serve with the flan. If it's a bit thick, thin it down with fresh milk to reach your preferred consistency.

Preheat the oven to 160°C on the combi steam setting with 30% moisture. Very lightly grease a shallow 23 cm round cake or fluted flan tin (the best way to do this is to use a paper towel dipped in a small amount of soft butter or vegetable oil). Place the tin on a baking tray.

For the chocolate flan, start by making a caramel. Place the caster sugar and water in a saucepan over an induction set on 8 or a gas burner over medium–high heat and bring to the boil until it starts to turn a golden colour. Remove from the heat once this colour is evenly distributed throughout the mixture.

Combine the milk, cream and cinnamon in a small saucepan and bring to the boil. Place the chocolate in a large stainless steel bowl. Pour the milk mixture over the chocolate and stir with a wooden spoon until the chocolate has melted completely and the mixture forms a rich chocolate sauce. Stir in the beaten egg, egg yolk and raw sugar until smooth.

Pour the caramel into the prepared tart tin and tilt the tin so it spreads evenly around the base. Pour the chocolate mixture gently over the top and bake for 50 minutes. By this time the tart will be shiny and firm, but still have wobble when moved. Place the flan in a cool place for 1 hour before demoulding onto a cake stand or platter. Decorate with chocolate curls and crumbs, and serve with the milk caramel on the side.

Note
To make chocolate curls, scrape a knife along the top of a block of chocolate, almost as if you are scraping butter. This will give a tight curl effect.

Visitor tips

Art galleries

Soumaya Gallery
Miguel de Cervantes Saavedra 303,
Granada, Miguel Hidalgo, 11529
☎ +52 55 1103 9800
soumaya.com.mx
An extraordinary building purpose-built
for the largest known private art collection
in Mexico, created by the richest man in
the world, Carlos Slim Helú, in honour of
his wife who passed away several years ago.
Slap-bang in the centre of Polanco.

Best margarita

Villa Maria
Av. Homero 704, Miguel Hidalgo,
Polanco, 11550
☎ +52 55 5203 0306
villamaria.com.mx
Frozen margaritas are the best! Try the
tamarindo and mango flavours. Ask for
the large; you only live once. In the
afternoon they have a mariachi show.

Markets

Coyoacan
Centro de Coyoacan,
Hidalgo & Malitzin, 04100
visitmexico.com/en/neighbordhood-
in-coyoacan-in-mexico-city
Great artisan market for gifts, especially
Mexican crafts.

Places of interest

Sun Pyramid
San Juan Teotihuacán, 55800
Teotihuacán de Arista
☎ +52 594 958 2081
This ancient Aztec pyramid is far from
the city, but the trip is worth it to learn
more about the Aztec culture.

Restaurants

Biko
Presidente Masaryk 407, Miguel Hidalgo,
Polanco, 11550
☎ +52 55 5282 2064
biko.com.mx
Mexico City's best restaurant. A must; be
sure to book well in advance. Conveniently
located in the Polanco area.

Cafe O
Monte Líbano 245, Lomas de
Chapultepec, Miguel Hidalgo, 11000,
Distrito Federal
☎ +52 55 5520 9227
onlyo.net
Chef Paola Garduño is amazing! Having
worked for four years with Danish chef
René Redzepi at Noma in Copenhagen,
Garduño is now turning her creative
knowledge to modern Mexican dishes with
the philosophy of less is more. You can see
the simple Noma techniques everywhere.

Restaurant Dulce Patria
Anatole France 100, Col. Polanco
☎ +52 55 3300 3999
dulcepatriamexico.com
The newest restaurant from chef Martha
Ortiz. Many locals say it is currently the
best representation of Mexican food in
the city. Fresh seafoods, fragrant chillies
and sauces and also great wines.

Restaurant Enrique
Avenida Insurgentes Sur 4061, 14000
☎ +52 55 5573 9988
Food that focuses on the central region of
Mexico, the Bajio. Dishes like taco placero,
guacamole with crispy broken shards of
pork skin and 'drink sauce', wrapped in
a tortilla; cactus salad; beans fried until
soft in pork fat; ram, cooked in the ground
wrapped in plantain leaves for hours; and
lamb soup with cilantro (coriander) and
raw onion. All the dishes come out in
a procession into the middle of the table,
like a do-it-yourself taco bar but with
serious passion.

Restaurant Pujol
Francisco Petrarca 254, Miguel Hidalgo,
Chapultepec Morales, 11570
☎ +52 55 5545 4111
pujol.com.mx
Food is of a very good standard and the
restaurant is working hard to preserve
the reputation of Mexican food as a serious
player in world cuisine. Be prepared for ten
courses with several choices within each.

Street food

El Huequito
Bolívar 58, Cuauhtémoc, Centro, 06000
☎ +52 55 5510 4199
elhuequito.com.mx
The king of tacos al pastor since 1959.
A Mexico City specialty, this is a shawarma-
like vertical spit of pork marinated with
dried chilli, then thinly sliced and rolled
into small, soft tortillas with chopped
onion and coriander.

Moscow

This city feels like something
from a fairytale, with colourful onion
domes on the churches everywhere.

I have had an epiphany: undertaking this trip is not mad. I am perhaps a romantic, foolish optimist, but not mad. Moscow, on the other hand, is completely bonkers! And I mean that in a good way. How do you sum up a city that has for many decades now defined the lives of so many beyond its borders, yet within, it feels like a manic beehive? Officially 15 million people live here; unofficially there are over 20 million. It's the food and the people I have come to see. Oh, and the little matter of cooking for a few guests, selling them on kangaroo and flogging some ovens.

The first step – getting through the airport – is a harrowing one. To start with, we somehow land at the wrong one, Sheremetyevo, when in fact it was meant to be the very large and nightmarish Domodedovo airport. I don't think it's the pilot's fault but it actually turned out to my advantage. I will explain.

I was informed by my Russian comrades – Sergey Kim, MD of Miele Russia, Irina the marketing director and Olga, head of Active Cooking, that it was unlikely at best that I'd be able to bring in the game meat I required. I was adamant, however, that the event had to include Australian ingredients or there was no point. I'm prepared to risk it. Cory and the team keep their distance as the bags and boxes come off the belt. With a slight twitch but an otherwise steely will, I squeeze my hand onto the release break of my trolley and push straight through. Ready to catch the eye of the first customs officer and plead my case, instead I'm waved away. I hurriedly push through the exit, job completed. The kangaroo has landed.

The only problem we now have to contend with is getting to the city. I'm warned that traffic is unpredictable and it can take quite a while to get to the hotel. I'm in good company, though – the team in Moscow are a lovely bunch. They also have to be resilient, with temperatures in the winter here dropping to -30°C! ➜

1–2 The Borodinsky Bridge.
3 The Orthodox Church, one of many in Moscow with the distinctive 'onion domes'.

Moscow is surrounded by three ring roads that encircle each other. The smallest is called the Garden Ring. They are all interlinked by smaller roads and this is where there is a traffic problem, with cars switching lanes and driving at all sorts of speeds without much regard for safety. Be well aware of this when crossing at traffic lights, where many drivers' inner maniac emerges. I did find the fact no one drinks and drives here fascinating and admirable, though. When I say no one I mean that; not even one little tipple. After many years of terrible consequences, the public and government took it upon themselves to take responsibility.

Four days in Moscow pass very quickly. The dinner launch and media appointments all go to plan, apart from me offending the most recognised food journalist and food critic in Moscow, Liudmila Salnikova. Her favourite restaurant in Moscow at the moment is White Rabbit. Not realising her enthusiasm for this establishment, I describe in detail how sad and ordinary I find it. Oops! I'm quick to smooth things over and by the time we have cooked for her I think she is sufficiently mollified.

Moscovians are a resilient bunch. Their history has so twisted their present; who knows what the following twenty years will bring them, but they are survivors. The oligarchs don't represent the new middle class here, in thoughts or ideals. What this country needs is time. I'd say don't come here for a foodie experience but rather a life one. Next time I will bring my children; it will show them how different we all are and that is what makes this world so exciting. ➔

4   A statue of Marshall Zhukov, one of Moscow's most famous military leaders, who was instrumental in the defeat of Hitler.

5   This statue of Peter the Great is also known not-so-fondly as 'The Terminator'. Debates rage constantly about whether to take it down.

6   A beautiful floral display at the Alexander Gardens, outside the Armoury Chamber at the Kremlin.

7   Soldiers outside the Kremlin.

8   The Horses Fountain in the Alexander Gardens.

Breakfast in Moscow

The cold temperatures are so extreme, the order of the day is hot, hearty food full of carbohydrates, such as thin and delicate mini-pancakes made from cottage cheese accompanying salted and smoked fish such as salmon, eel or kippers. Jams are works of art in this part of the world; unusual berries are used in inspired combinations that prove irresistible when spread over those pancakes. Porridge is also a staple, along with stewed fruits.

Did you know?

What we know as Russian salad is actually called 'Olivier salad' in Russia. It's named after its creator, a Belgian chef; this dish is traditionally served during the new year. Christmas celebrations were banned during the Soviet era and are only slowly making a comeback, but Russians really celebrate the new year and no party is complete without this salad. ●

9–10   The Annunciation Cathedral of Moscow. The city glitters with gold domes such as these, giving it an instantly recognisable character.

11   It's traditional for newlyweds to come to the Alexander Gardens and have their pictures taken. This Moscow bride sensibly accessorises with a practical yet glamorous warm shrug.

12   Another view of the Alexander Gardens.

Smoked salmon eggs
with egg cream

Serves 4

Russians prefer salmon eggs to caviar, and I tend to agree with their preference. In Melbourne we are very lucky to have the Yarra Valley salmon farm. Nick from the farm demonstrated to us how to milk a salmon then return it to the lake unharmed. The maturity in the flavour was sensational. Adding smoke gives this dish another layer.

120 g salted salmon eggs
3 tablespoons wood chips (preferably tea tree
or untreated pine)
8 pieces wafer-thin lavosh or ultra-thin
croutons
sprig tea tree or pine, to garnish

Egg cream
4 eggs
40 g carrot, peeled, chopped, cooked
and pureed
2 tablespoons apple vinegar
25 ml chicken glaze (made by simply reducing
75 ml chicken stock to 25 ml)
200 ml vegetable oil
1 slice fresh white bread, crusts
removed (optional)
sea salt
lemon juice, to taste

To make the egg cream, cook the eggs for 6 minutes in a steamer at 100% steam. Set aside to cool, then peel. Blend the eggs, carrot, vinegar and chicken glaze with a stick blender to make a paste, then slowly blend in the oil until thick and creamy. If it is not thick enough for your liking, blend in the white bread. Season to taste with salt and lemon juice. Transfer the mixture to a piping bag or sauce bottle and leave to the side.

To smoke the salmon eggs, line a baking tray with baking paper. Place the eggs on one half of the tray, and the wood chips on the other half. Take a blowtorch or brulee burner and torch the chips until they turn red, then place the tray in a well-sealed oven and leave for 10 minutes (without turning the oven on). This process has to be done at the last minute.

To serve, pipe or pour the egg cream onto a serving plate or board, add the salmon eggs and garnish with a sprig of tea tree or pine. Using a blowtorch, burn the top of the sprig just before serving to create a smoky atmosphere. Serve with lavosh or croutons on the side.

Paprika chicken casserole

Serves 4

I literally had to pick myself up off the floor when I paid $90 US for a French corn-fed chicken. For this sort of money the dish has to be memorable, so I have taken inspiration from tabaco, a well-known local dish roasted with a brick and chilli flakes. If you can, start the recipe the day before you need it so the chicken can marinate overnight.

1 tablespoon sweet paprika
pinch of saffron threads
2 teaspoon chilli flakes
1 teaspoon crushed red peppercorns
4 large cloves garlic, crushed
¼ cup (60 ml) extra virgin olive oil
1 × 2 kg free-range chicken, butterflied (ask your poultry supplier to do this for you)
2 onions, peeled, cut in half and thinly sliced
2 red capsicums (peppers), cut in half, seeds and membranes removed and cut into 1 cm thick slices
2 yellow capsicums (peppers), cut in half, seeds and membranes removed and cut into 1 cm thick slices
2 cups (220 g) girolles or small button mushrooms, wiped clean
1 litre chicken stock
5 spring onions
sea salt

Combine the spices, garlic and 2 tablespoons olive oil in a ceramic bowl. Add the chicken and turn to coat well, then cover and marinate in the fridge for at least 1 hour, or preferably overnight.

Preheat the oven on intensive bake to 160°C.

Heat the remaining olive oil in a large flameproof casserole dish over an induction set on 5 or a gas burner over medium heat, add the onion and red and yellow capsicum and saute for 3–4 minutes. Add the mushrooms and cook for 1 minute, then add the stock and bring to the boil.

Place the chicken in the dish and return to a simmer, then cover the dish with a lid. Transfer to the oven and bake for 30 minutes. Check if the chicken is cooked by inserting a knife into the thickest part – if the juices run clear, it's ready. Arrange the spring onions over the chicken and serve. This goes particularly well with pickled cabbage salad (see right).

Pickled cabbage salad

Serves 4

My motivation for including this recipe was our visit to the very famous Eliseevskiy food store, where they sell this salad by the tub. A little tip here is to strain beetroot juice from tinned beetroot and use it to intensify the flavour and colour of the dish.

2 banana shallots, cut in half, peeled and roughly chopped (use golden shallots if unavailable)
180 ml white wine vinegar
180 g honey
400 ml wheat beer or water
1 teaspoon each caraway seeds, mustard seeds and fennel seeds, wrapped in a piece of cheese cloth.
1 small purple cabbage, cut into 8 wedges

Combine the shallot, vinegar, honey, beer or water and bundle of seeds in a medium saucepan and bring to the boil. Add the cabbage, then remove from the heat and cover with a lid. Leave in the fridge for several hours, or preferably overnight, before serving.

Russian honey cake

Serves 8

I'm sure this is one of the most overused lines
by men, but I'm not really a cake lover. At least
I thought I wasn't. This recipe has changed my
mind, with its fine layers of delicate sponge
and rich honey cream. As most pastry chefs are
aware, making honey the 'hero' of a recipe can be
challenging, but this cake does just that: it makes
the sponge speak of honey.

1 cup (220 g) brown sugar
2 eggs, lightly beaten
135 g cultured butter
2 tablespoons honey
2 teaspoons baking powder
3 cups (450 g) plain flour, plus extra if needed
icing sugar, for dusting

Honey cream filling
1 × 395 g can sweetened condensed milk
3 eggs, lightly beaten
2 tablespoons honey
150 g cultured butter

Start by preparing the honey cream filling. Pour
the condensed milk into a large saucepan over an
induction set on 7 or a gas burner over medium heat
and bring to a simmer. Remove from the heat, add
the egg, honey and butter and whisk until smooth
and well combined. Return the pan to the heat, this
time over an induction set on 4, and bring to the
boil, whisking constantly until the mixture thickens.
Transfer to a bowl, cover with plastic film and leave
to cool completely at room temperature.

Preheat the oven on intensive bake to 180°C.
Grease and line a 20–24 cm springform cake tin
and lightly flour 3 baking sheets. Cut 5 sheets of
baking paper into circles the same size as your
cake tin.

Using an electric mixer, whisk the brown
sugar and eggs until pale and fluffy. Melt the
butter in a large saucepan over low heat. Add the
honey and stir to combine, then add to the egg
mixture and whisk for several minutes until well
emulsified. Add the baking powder and stir until
well blended and foamy.

Sift the flour into the mixer bowl, change
the whisk to a dough hook and mix on slow until
a light dough is formed. If the dough is still quite
sticky add a little extra flour. Divide the dough
into 5 equal portions and place on the baking paper
circles; cover each dough portion with plastic film
to keep the warmth in.

Starting with 3 portions of dough, roll it out
with a floured rolling pin to a 5 mm thick round.
Place the rounds on the prepared baking sheets
and bake on all 3 shelves for 6 minutes or until
light golden. Keep a close eye on them as they
are easy to overcook. Remove from the oven and
cool completely on wire racks. Repeat with the
remaining 2 portions of dough.

To assemble the cake, place the first layer of
sponge in the prepared cake tin and spread with
a quarter of the honey cream. Continue layering,
finishing with the final layer of cake. Garnish with
any sponge crumbs you have left over, then sift
icing sugar liberally over the top. Rest in the fridge
for 2 hours, then gently loosen the side of the tin
and transfer the cake to a serving plate or cake
stand. Cut into wedges to serve.

Visitor tips

Getting around

The Metro network in Moscow is safe and efficient but be warned, it's noisy. It accesses some of the oldest stations around the Kremlin area; they are architectural masterpieces, with Ploshchad Revolyutsii, Kievskaya and Komsomolskaya really standing out. I was advised to take a local with me; thank my lucky stars that I listened to this advice. The Russian language is not only hard to speak, but also there is little chance of me being able to learn the Cyrillic alphabet any time soon!

Art and architecture

Christ Our Saviour Cathedral
Ulitsa Volkhonka 15, 119019
☎ +7 495 637 12 76
xxc.ru
This cathedral, the biggest in Moscow, was originally constructed in the nineteenth century. It was destroyed during the 1930s, when Stalin ordered it to be demolished. He then commissioned an enormous statue to be erected on the site but due to the wet, unstable ground on the banks of the Moscow river, ended up building a heated public swimming pool. This became one of the most well-known landmarks in all of Moscow. In the mid-nineties, the church was resurrected as an exact replica and fully rebuilt with donated money. An awe-inspiring experience both inside and out.

The Pushkin Gallery
Ulitsa Volkhonka 12, 119019
☎ +7 495 697 95 78
www.arts-museum.ru
The largest permanent exhibition of European art in Russia. Built in 1912, the gallery is extremely popular and lines extend around the corner on most days. To avoid the queue, arrive at 10 a.m. when the doors open. Allow yourself at least two hours. The 'private collection' houses the greatest collection of Impressionists and post-Impressionists I have ever viewed under one roof – Dunard, Guigan, Monet, Matisse and Picasso.

St Basil's Cathedral
Krasnaya Ploshad, 109012
☎ +7 495 698 33 04
saintbasil.ru
Famous for the colourful onion-shaped turrets on Red Square, close to Lenin's tomb. One of the most famous landmarks in the world.

The State Tretyakov Gallery
Lavrushinskiy Pereulok 10, 119017
☎ +7 499 230 77 88
tretyakovgallery.ru
Also worth a visit. It houses a huge collection of Russian works; allow at least half a day here.

Bars

Luch Bar
Ulitsa Bolshaya Pirogovskaya, 27
☎ +7 495 287 00 22
luchbar.ru
The best decor of any bar in Moscow, set in an old lightbulb factory. Art, cocktails and the beautiful people combine in a vast, well-appointed 'less is more; let the contemporary art do the talking' space. Wild herbs are used (wildly) in the cocktails, and there's an extensive list of whiskys. Bar food is worth trying.

Mendeleev
Petrovka Street, House 20/1
☎ +7 495 625 33 85
Looking for a nightcap while slipping under the tourist radar? Check out a bar called Mendeleev. It's just up the road from the Ararat Park Hyatt. You enter via the Lucky Noodle shop and go through the black curtain, then downstairs. Great cocktails.

O2 Bar and Lounge
Tverskaya Street 3, 125009
☎ +7 495 225 88 88
ritzcarlton.com
Half stylish Japanese restaurant, half trendy pre-club hangout. Located on the twelfth floor of the Ritz Carlton with outstanding views over Moscow.

Strelka Institute/Bar
14 Bersenevskaya Embankment Building 5A, 119072
☎ +7 495 771 74 16
strelkainstitute.com/bar
The Red October chocolate factory, now converted into an entertainment complex with bars, cafes and art galleries, has views over Moscow River. One of Moscow's hottest spots to have a drink.

Coffee

Coffee Mania
13 Bolshaya Nikitskaya Street
☎ **+7 495 775 51 88**
coffeemania.ru
This is a chain of upmarket shops that sell
pretty decent freshly roasted espresso and
filter coffees. Be warned, a cup of coffee will
set you back at least double what you'd pay
in most other cities.

Hotels

Ararat Park Hyatt
4 Neglinnaya St, 109012
☎ **+7 495 783 12 34**
moscow.park.hyatt.com
A five-minute stroll to the Red Square,
the KGB building and the Bolshoi theatre,
this hotel whispers discreet luxury.
Standard rooms are generously sized with
large bathrooms and separate showers.
The rooftop bar, Bibliotheque, has an
outside deck overlooking some of
Moscow's most famous landmarks.

Golden Apple Hotel
Ulitsa Malaya Dmitrovka, 11, 127006
☎ **+7 495 980 70 00**
goldenapple.ru
One of the only true boutique hotels in
Moscow. Rooms are small but nicely
appointed. The clientele is an alternative,
arty crowd unique to Moscow.

Provedores

A great way to discover a country's food is to go and scout around the city's best supermarket or food hall. Here is where you discover the true fabric of the food culture. Most inner-city Moscow supermarkets offer a huge, good-quality range of meats, fish and vegetables, but they are all imported. With years of Soviet rule behind them, people want brand names. I think Moscow's best food actually comes from countries on its outer borders, such as Georgia, Armenia and Kazakhstan.

Eliseevskiy Food Store
Ulitsa Tverskaya, 14
☎ +7 495 650 46 43
eliseevskiy.ru/e_home.htm
Opened before the Russian Revolution of 1917 by millionaire Grigory Eliseev. The food is reasonable but really, go to look at the interior; the architecture is mind-bogglingly beautiful. Prices are unbelievable. We're talking US$50 for a fresh chicken, and if you buy French chickens, they will set you back over US$80 each!

Restaurants

Bolshoi Cafe
Petrovka Street, House 3/6, Structure 2, 125009
☎ +7 495 789 86 52
novikovgroup.ru/
White linen tablecloths, silver service, large wine list, and a grand setting in a grand location. Yes, this restaurant ticks all the boxes, but I didn't think the food was really anything special. Order simply.

Cafe Pushkin
Tverskoy Bul 26a
☎ +7 495 739 00 33
cafe-pushkin.ru
A replica grand old mansion converted into a restaurant. The bar and downstairs areas are packed with atmosphere, but it's undeniably a tourist venue. The food can be overly elaborate and not that great – probably best just to stick with a pastry and coffee. And try the house-made kvas, a non-alcoholic drink extracted from fermented black bread. Go to say you've been.

Sakhli
Bolshoy Karetniy Pereulok 6/1, 127051
☎ +7 495 699 45 03
sakhli.ru
The best Georgian food in the capital. It's hard to find – use a driver. The basement restaurant has live music blaring, and the atmosphere is hazy and noisy. No tourists here. The menu is packed with traditional dishes such as eggplant doused in walnut sauce, a delicious red bean stew, brown trout with herb sauce, and slices of veal sauteed with fresh tomatoes, herbs and spices. The real highlight has to be *hinkali*, a dumpling filled with juicy minced lamb. Make sure you try the desserts. And a word of warning – smoking in most restaurants is permitted anywhere! This is a problem for many diners, but if you can tolerate the haze and the reminder on your clothes the next day, I highly recommend this place.

← **Shinok**
Ulitsa 1905 Goda 2
☎ +7 495 651 81 01
shinok.ru
A very famous Ukrainian restaurant on the outskirts of the city centre. Ignore the greeting you receive from the funereal owner downstairs upon arrival. The menu is simple but interesting – for example, chicken smoked with hay and shasliks in all different forms. I go for a platter of cured meats and lardo with pickles. It's really good: smoky and salty with intense flavour.

Turandot
Tverskoy Bul 26/5
☎ +7 495 739 00 11
turandotpalace.ru
A few doors down from Cafe Pushkin, the dining room here is spectacular. The food is good, but that's not really the point. This is a place to see and be seen in.

Vatrushka
Bolshaya Nikitskaya Street, House 5, 125009
☎ +7 495 530 55 11
Interesting modern Soviet cuisine, famous for pancakes with salmon roe and smoked salmon in opulent surrounds.

White Rabbit
Smolenskaya Square 3
☎ +7 495 663 39 99
whiterabbitmoscow.ru
The hottest restaurant in Moscow right now, perched on the sixteenth floor of a luxury shopping centre. It's near-impossible to make a reservation for dinner; lunch is much easier. The view from the outdoor deck, across Moscow centre and over the Moscow river to the Red Square, cannot be beaten. I have the distinct feeling that the owners know this, and are prepared to rest on their laurels, as the fit-out in general is way too tacky, while the menu is unexciting.

Russian baths

Sanduny Baths
Neglinnaya ulitsa, 14
☎ +7 495 625 46 33
sanduny.ru
This unique bathing centre combines tradition with luxury. You may see the odd famous actor or oligarch here. The 40°C steam rooms and bathtubs are so relaxing and very Russian. I think there is no better way to understand this city than to have a traditional banya.

Nice

A city by the sea, watched over
by King Neptune, where it's
all about sailing and seafood.

We've booked in to the Negresco: Nice's world-famous, legendary hotel. France is a hard market for kitchen appliance companies to succeed in, especially since the GFC. Like most of Europe, Miele has an uncompromising reputation of 'Only the best will do' with the wealthy demographic. No disrespect to this class of person but they are normally the ones who actually have the least time or inclination to get home and cook! France, I would suspect, has a common theme uniting all demographics: 'I love to cook and I love to eat, so I need the best to achieve this.'

Ego is a powerful thing, and I think I'll be up against it with the France Miele team. Why would they want an Australian upstart chef coming over and preaching to the converted? It is like the chief of race engineering at Holden going over to Ferrari and telling them how to build a super car!

Suffice to say, I had been warned. To my surprise, the team met us at the airport. Gustav Schütz, the head of Miele France and a Sir Laurence Olivier lookalike, is a well spoken, witty and very knowledgable gentleman. The other was Franck, a young guy studying his masters of business as well as looking after the Nice Gallery as Gustav's deputy. Both men were welcoming and friendly and I even detected a touch of excitement. This warm greeting with huge smiles and open arms by such elegant and refined gentlemen was the last thing I expected, but more surprises awaited us.

We arrive at the small Nice Gallery, located on the west side of the promenade, conveniently close to the airport to find a brand-spanking-new showroom. My praise hits the spot, and Franck tells me we are going to be the first to use the space, as it is not officially open as yet. ➔

1   The Galerie Lapita, which houses a fine collection of Oceanic art.
2   Grand European architecture with palm trees and sandy beaches in the distance – Nice offers the best of two worlds.
3   The view from our hotel window.
4   L'Escalinada, a restaurant known and loved throughout the region for its traditional fare.
5   The Hotel de Paris, which has featured in many films, including *The Red Shoes* and several James Bond movies.

Franck then takes us on a tour of Nice. It is great getting his thoughts on a city he knows intimately. He agrees that it is a town you live in, rather than visit.

There's a sense of freedom, especially in the old town. Passing through the main gates just off the main corniche, one is transported back to the Moorish days of medieval Europe. I would enjoy a ramble, sipping sweet coffee in traditional cafes amid locals going about their business and a scattering of tourists. Oh, the joy of a tourist destination that doesn't have many tourists! The style of the old town is reminiscent of the old fort in Galle, Sri Lanka. Outside its walls are the busy promenade of St Angliss to the south and to the north the rocky outcrops and the arterial road linking this area to the wonders of the Cote d'Azur.

Food culture in the area is heavily influenced by Italy. Pasta, Menton lemons, aromatic herbs, tomatoes, eggplants and zucchini are all intertwined with more classical, well-known French dishes, resulting in food that is light, fresh and healthy. Walk into a bakery here and you find the bread even looks more Italian in style. The most notable difference is olive oil; it replaces butter in almost all dishes and even at the table. Olive trees grow in profusion. ➜

6

6   The harbour at Nice.
7   Our host Franck organises for us to pop in and see one of Miele's most loyal customers, former racing car driver, Yves Saguato. We meet on the boat he and his wife cruise around the world on, fully decked out in Miele marine state-of-the-art equipment.
8   A statue of trumpeter Miles Davis by sculptor Niki de St Phalle.

Over the past decades African culture has also worked its way into recipes, with aromatic spices and even chilli being added to classic cassoulet, for example.

Fresh seafood is not what it once was in the region, with over-fishing meaning that certain species indigenous to the area are no longer easily found at the fishmongers. John Dory and rouget (red mullet) are still common, but scorpion fish and local lobsters are harder to come by. Silverbeet is in everything; the locals call it blette.

One thing this part of the world still does incredibly well that my home country could learn a lot from is celebrate the seasons. In all the fruit shops I walk past in the old town, *fraises des bois* (wild strawberries) are in abundance, yet I cannot see an apple for sale anywhere.

The three Miele team members we have been given are very new to their positions so this puts us behind the eight ball. The kangaroo has arrived, but obviously it is sacrilegious to even think that we should use barramundi so local sea bass is a perfect substitution. ●

9   The Apollo Neptune statue at Place Masséna.
10 A view of the boats at the marina, with the mountains rising up majestically beyond.
11 The side entrance to the Monte Carlo Casino and Opera House.
12 Monte Carlo Casino and Opera House.

Socca

Serves 4

Socca is a Provencal pancake made from chickpea flour. I think it makes a great entree for any dinner party – the degree of difficulty is not huge, and the pancakes are a terrific base upon which to add creative toppings, such as marinated mackerel and strips of roast capsicum. Or you can just enjoy them as they are traditionally served along the Côte d'Azur, as a type of bread for dips such as tapenade.

2 cups (300 g) chickpea flour
2 cups (500 ml) water
2 tablespoons olive oil, plus extra for cooking
1 teaspoon sea salt
freshly ground black pepper

Preheat the oven on fan grill to 280°C.

Mix together the flour, water, olive oil, salt and pepper and pass through a fine-mesh sieve.

Pour 1 tablespoon extra olive oil into a non-stick pizza tray and tilt the tray so it covers the base. Ladle one quarter of the batter into the tray and spread it around like a crepe.

Transfer to the oven and bake for 8 minutes or until golden brown and starting to blister. Take out the tray and add flavourings if you like, or just a sprinkling of salt, then cut into rough pieces and serve warm. Repeat with the remaining batter to make 4 pancakes in all.

Pan-roasted red mullet with charred leeks and sauteed blette

Serves 4

Red mullet is found in oceans all around the world. It needs to be eaten as fresh as possible, as the stomach deteriorates quickly, and I find the best fishmongers will leave it intact and unscaled on display, ready to be enjoyed on the day it is caught.

Perhaps better known as silverbeet or chard, blette leaves are the hero of the dish, cooked in goose fat with shallot, garlic and anchovies. (The stems can be used delicately on their own, simply peeled, steamed and served in batons.) The resulting mixture can be used in egg dishes, as a pastry filling, or shaped into quenelles and served with meat or fish.

4 baby leeks, well washed, excess root
 trimmed off
2 tablespoons olive oil
4 × 250 g red mullets, cleaned and scaled
40 g butter
juice of ½ lemon
1 tablespoon roughly chopped
 flat-leaf parsley

Mustard foam
300 ml grapeseed oil
3 small eggs
3 large egg yolks
1 egg white
1 medium potato, steamed, peeled and mashed
 while still hot
25 ml white wine vinegar
1 teaspoon sea salt
1 tablespoon Dijon mustard

Sauteed blette
1 tablespoon goose fat or olive oil
1 golden shallot, peeled, cut in half and
 finely diced
½ clove garlic, minced
1 bunch blettes or silverbeet (leaves only),
 washed, blanched for 2 minutes,
 then finely chopped
3 salted Ortiz anchovies, finely crushed
sea salt

Preheat the oven to fan grill on 225°C.

To make the mustard foam, pour all the ingredients into a saucepan and gently warm up over low heat for 1 minute, whisking constantly – do not let it boil. Pour into a cream whip gun and place the lid on. Charge with 2 gas bulbs and shake well.

For the sauteed blette, heat the goose fat or olive oil in a small heavy-based saucepan over an induction set on 2 or a gas burner over low heat. Add the shallot and garlic and saute for 2 minutes or until softened but not coloured. Add the blette or silverbeet and anchovies and saute for about 2 minutes until the anchovies have started to melt. Season to taste with salt.

Place the leeks on a baking tray and cook in the oven for 6 minutes or until nicely charred. (You could also cook them on a charcoal barbecue, if preferred.) Cover and keep warm.

Preheat the oven on the conventional setting to 160°C.

Heat the olive oil in a large ovenproof non-stick frying pan over an induction set on 7 or a gas burner over medium–high heat. Fry the fish for 4 minutes or until the skin is crisp and golden, then turn the fish over and place in the oven for 4 minutes. Remove the fish and rest in a warm place. Return the pan to the stovetop, add the butter, lemon juice and parsley and melt over medium heat.

Baste the fish with the pan juices. Place the fish on warm plates, along with the leeks, sauteed blette and mustard foam to serve.

Choux pastries with pistachio cream

Serves 4

Choux pastry is the standard test of a good pastry chef, and much of its success relies on the quality of the oven. The Miele 'moisture plus' function certainly helps here. Nice is heaven on earth for pistachio lovers – you can buy them fresh, roasted in the shell and in paste form from any reasonable fruit shop. Combine crisp choux buns with pistachio cream, lemon zest and fresh strawberries for the ultimate pastry pleasure.

finely grated lemon zest and fresh strawberries, to serve

Choux pastries
1 cup (250 ml) water
125 g butter, cut into small pieces
pinch of sea salt
1⅔ cups (250 g) plain flour, sifted
6 eggs, lightly beaten
100 g hazelnuts, roasted, skins removed and crushed

Pistachio cream
200 g shelled pistachios
100 g unsalted roasted almonds
200 ml cream
¼ cup (55 g) caster sugar

Preheat the oven on the conventional setting to 170°C. Line 2 baking trays with baking paper.

To make the choux pastry, combine the water, butter and salt in a large heavy-based saucepan and heat over an induction set on 2. When all the butter has melted, increase the induction to 7 until the mixture boils, stirring occasionally. When the mixture comes to the boil, take the pan off the heat, add the flour and mix with a wooden spoon until combined.

Return the pan to induction 5 for about 2 minutes, stirring constantly, until the mixture comes together and starts to leave the side of the pan. Transfer the dough to an electric mixer fitted with the paddle attachment and mix for a few minutes until the dough is no longer steaming hot, but is still warm.

Gradually add the egg, making sure each addition is fully incorporated before adding the next. Scrape down the side of the bowl to ensure the dough is silky, smooth and uniform. Transfer the dough to a piping bag fitted with a large plain nozzle and pipe your desired shapes onto the prepared baking trays. Immediately sprinkle over the crushed hazelnuts and bake for 20–30 minutes or until golden. Remove from the oven and cool completely on the trays.

Meanwhile, to make the pistachio cream, scatter the pistachios and almonds into a dry frying pan and roast over medium heat for 2 minutes. Keep a close eye on them as they burn easily. Transfer the warm nuts to a food processor and blitz to form a smooth paste (scrape down the side of the bowl as needed). Set aside to cool in a mixing bowl.

Once cool, lightly whip the cream and sugar together to 'ribbon' stage. Gently fold one third of the cream into the nut paste, then gently fold in the rest. Cover and store in the fridge until you are ready to serve.

Finely grate lemon zest over the pastries and serve with strawberries and the pistachio cream.

Visitor tips

Hotels

Le Negresco ↓
37 Promenade des Anglais, 06000
☎ +33 4 93 16 64 00
hotel-negresco-nice.com

Le Negresco has always been on my bucket list. Anyone who is anyone has stayed in this hotel. I feel as if I'm in one of Peter Sellers' Pink Panther flicks. It's ramshackle and charming in a seventies time-warp sort of way – my bed was in the shape of a turtle shell! Stay here for fun without expectations.

Restaurants

Mirazur →
30 Avenue Aristide Briand, 06500 Menton
☎ +33 4 92 41 86 86
mirazur.fr

The picturesque surrounds of Menton is the setting for the world-renowned Mirazur restaurant. The restaurant setting and aesthetics is all about the view, which is directed towards Monaco. It is stunning. Creative snacks such as logs topped with moss, with green powder-dusted mushrooms. Vegetables picked from the gardens below the restaurant are stuffed with tuna and served with a delicious salty anchovy sauce.

Prague

A fresh take on traditional Czech
food which makes the most of wild
ingredients in season - game,
berries and mushrooms.

My first thirty minutes in Prague is a blur. All I can remember is a brutally handsome Czech bloke named Tomàs Abraham, managing director of Miele in the region, welcoming me with a beaming smile.

I'm staying at the Mandarin Oriental, but there's barely time to check in. The Miele team is waiting for me out the front of the hotel when I arrive. 'Hey Bennett', someone shouts energetically. This is my introduction to chef Radek Subrt. Tomas has organised Radek, host and judge of the local version of *Masterchef*, and his sidekick Martin, to help us find the ingredients for the promotional dinner we are putting on at the Prague Miele Gallery in just over twenty-four hours.

Radek grabs my hand, moulds it into an arm-wrestle-type grip and smiles at me silently. The whole team crams into Radek's van and we're off. It feels as if the Great Race has begun.

Hostin

We quickly leave the cobblestoned roads and masses of incredible buildings and are soon driving through picturesque country lanes and roads. I have no idea where we are going, but no matter.

One hour later, we pull up at Maxmilián Game Farm in the small village of Hostin, owned by a local millionaire who loves hunting. He bought the land surrounding the village and turned it back into forest, complete with a hunting lodge, game-processing plant and private museum.

Then it is off to the museum. The first stuffed animal that catches my eye is a Bengal tiger. Carefully stroking it, the guide claims the animal passed away peacefully at the local zoo before being transferred to the game farm's dining room. I wonder, though: what is the small bullet-hole-sized scar on the left side of its neck?

Everywhere I look there are stuffed animals, from elephants, giraffes, wolves, lynxes and coyotes to masses of birds. The walls are covered with deer heads and the occasional buffalo. I'm assuming *Dances with Wolves* was never translated into Czech. A solitary dining table with zebra-skin-covered chairs is set in the centre of all this carnage. →

1   My first view of Prague.
2–4   At Maximilián Game Farm.

I have only been in the Czech Republic for two hours at this stage. By now we are behind schedule and this seems to excite Radek. We race down the narrow lanes until we reach some large lush green fields in a small valley. A very attractive woman stares at us, wearing nothing but a zebra-striped bikini. That seems to be the theme around here. She gets all our attention until a local farmer walks towards us with a beaming smile. He takes us on a tour to pick some herbs, new potatoes and some greens for our planned recipe-testing tonight.

Radek uses the word 'quickly' in every sentence, and if I use it to describe how we arrived back in Malá Strana, that's an understatement.

Twenty minutes later, showered, hair still dishevelled, hungry and jetlagged, I walk with Tomàs and the team through the Presidential Palace Square overlooking Prague to our restaurant at the foot of the South Gardens, Terasa U Zlaté Studne.

The restaurant is full of tourists – Tomàs says this is where you take friends and business associates from overseas to impress them.

'So, what is Czech food?' I ask Tomàs. 'Steak with cream sauce,' he replies. I'm a little saddened by the response, but later learn that *Svíčková na smetane* (marinated sirloin with braised vegetables and cream, served with bread dumplings) is one of the Czech Republic's classic dishes.

They eat well in this town: wild mushrooms, wild game, abundant fresh vegetables, dumplings, and freshwater fish from the Vltava and its surrounding lakes.

I finally check into my hotel at around midnight, after nearly forty hours without sleep. Press interviews start at 9 a.m. and I have the Miele media dinner for thirty people tomorrow.

Asian food is starting to show its face in Prague in a big way. Tomàs's favourite little eatery is SaSaZu, in the warehouse district. The chef is an Israeli guy cooking Vietnamese food in a place attached to a nightclub, and you can have a massage after your meal. ➔

5–6   Picking herbs with a local farmer to use as garnish for the Miele gala dinner.

7–8   New potatoes and lettuces from the region.

9–10 The view from our restaurant, Terasa U Zlaté Studně.

11   St George's Basilica.

12   A guard at the Gate of Giants, opening on to Castle Square.

13   The Charles Bridge across the Vltava River.

14   A stroll through the centre of town is like stepping back in time several hundred years.

For my part, I'm still on a mission to get to a definition of Czech food. The answer is closer, but I still need to dig deeper. There is more to this country than goulash (*gulás*), dumplings (*knedlíky*), and braised meats with mushrooms and cream. So far, I have discovered wild herbs, eight varieties of honey, the importance of organics, local fruits made into preserves and more varieties of jam than I've ever seen anywhere else, wild mountain goats, wild ducks, many varieties of wild mushrooms, wild garlic flowers and river fish.

We then race across the city to have coffee on the twenty-seventh floor of a skyscraper on Prague's outskirts, where Aureole has opened. The view is breathtaking and we take a moment to relax in the all-white lounge. But soon it is back in the van so that Tomàs can show us more of Prague.

For dinner, it is off to one of the hottest restaurants in town: La Dégustation Bohême Bourgeoise. But as we have five minutes to spare, Tomàs takes us for a calming beer at Kolkovna, a traditional Czech pub.

After ordering us massive jugs of Czech beer, Tomàs insists that we have a few snacks to help the beer down and orders lean brawn with onions and vinegar and some spicy pickled sausages. He also shows great skill in getting everyone's beer replaced without them noticing. ●

15   The public Vrtba Gardens. These baroque terraced gardens flow across the gradient of the hill, filled with miniature hedged mazes.

16   The team settle down for a typical Czech lunch before Tomàs, seated second left, takes us on a dash across the city for coffee.

17   Locals enjoying a drink at Mercato bar.

18   St Vitus Cathedral.

19–20   St Salvator Church, part of the Klementinum (the Czech Jesuit College), and its ancient surrounding streets.

21   'Love locks' on the Charles Bridge. Lovers fix a padlock to the bridge to symbolise their commitment to one another.

Braised beef cheeks

Serves 4

The Czechs have a strong attachment to their cuisine. They do not hide away from the similarities to other neighbouring countries such as Hungary, hence the goulash is a dish shared by both cultures. This warming winter dish is deeply ensconced in the culinary traditions of every family, but strangely it is also something many people order when dining out at traditional eating houses. Beef cheeks are one of 12 cuts used for this dish; their dense, unctuous characteristics are perfect for the long braising time needed to bring out the subtle chilli and cumin flavours. Beer is the drink of choice when eating this dish but the wines from the Moravian Valley are now starting to gain a reputation – ironically more with foodie tourists than with Prague locals.

2 tablespoons olive oil
4 × 350 g beef cheeks, trimmed of excess fat
sea salt
4 medium brown onions, cut in half, peeled
    and thinly sliced
1 tablespoon cumin seeds, toasted and ground
1 carrot, peeled and cut in half
½ head garlic, peeled and sliced
2 large red chillies, seeded and
    roughly chopped
1 litre tomato passata
1 litre chicken stock
2 teaspoons smoked paprika
2 pickled onions (see page 195), cut into rings

Bacon dumplings
1 sandwich loaf, crusts removed, cut into
    small cubes
200 g smoked bacon, cut into small cubes
100 g smoked pork fat, cut into small cubes
4 egg whites
pinch of sea salt
splash of milk (optional)

Preheat the oven to 150°C on the combi steam setting with 20% moisture.

Heat the olive oil in a flameproof casserole dish over high heat. Season the beef cheeks with salt, then add to the casserole and cook for 1 minute on each side. Add the onion and cumin, then reduce the heat to medium and cook for 3 minutes. Add the carrot, garlic and chilli and mix together, then pour in the tomato passata and chicken stock. Place the casserole in the oven and cook for 6 hours.

Remove the casserole from the oven and rest the cheeks in the cooking liquid for about 30 minutes. To test whether the beef cheeks are cooked, pull a piece of flesh with a spoon – it should come apart with ease.

Meanwhile, to make the dumplings, preheat the oven on the conventional setting to 180°C. Spread out the bread cubes on a baking tray and bake for 10 minutes or until golden. Place the bacon and pork fat in a frying pan and cook over an induction set on 8 or a gas burner over medium–high heat for 1 minute. Remove from the pan and drain on paper towel. Whisk the egg whites until soft peaks form. Combine the bacon, pork, bread cubes and salt in a bowl, then fold in the egg whites. Add a splash of milk if the mixture is not holding together. Leave to sit for 10 minutes.

Tear off a piece of plastic film about 50 cm in length and place on a flat surface. Spoon the dumpling mixture along the edge closest to you in a sausage shape, then roll up firmly in the plastic film, making sure there are no air pockets. Secure each end with the excess plastic film, then steam for 25 minutes or until cooked through. Carefully remove the plastic film and cut into discs of your desired thickness.

Transfer the beef cheeks to a plate and cover to keep warm. Using a stick blender or regular blender, process the cooking juices and vegetables together to form a thick sauce. Return the beef cheeks to the sauce and reheat briefly in the oven.

Place the beef cheeks in individual bowls and spoon the sauce over the top. Serve with the dumplings and pickled onion rings.

New potato salad

Serves 4

With the rise of farmers' markets one ingredient I get really excited about is freshly dug-up potatoes. At certain times of the year, it is reasonable to expect that potatoes have been stored in dark cold rooms before being sold at market, but small new potatoes from local markets are the exception. It doesn't matter about the variety – all that matters is the freshness.

The farm Radek took us to was predominately a potato and lettuce farm, which inspired this recipe: my take on potato salad, a national summer staple in Prague. It's served with everything, as an entree, as a side dish or even as a light meal, always with grated vegetables and bound with mayonnaise.

My version relies heavily on a delicious egg emulsion recipe – a puree of cooked egg, vegetables and apple vinegar. Because of its texture, you can dress it up by serving it piped, or just mix it all together in a more relaxed fashion. The egg emulsion is also great as a dip, in sandwiches or served with vegetables and other salads. It will keep in the fridge for several days.

8 small breakfast radishes
8 baby new potatoes
1 tablespoon melted butter
salt flakes
⅓ cup (55 g) fresh peas
dandelion leaves, refreshed in ice cold water,
    to garnish (optional)

Egg emulsion
5 eggs
20 g carrot, peeled, roughly chopped and
    boiled or steamed until tender
20 g celeriac, peeled, roughly chopped and
    boiled or steamed until tender
1 tablespoon apple vinegar
25 ml chicken glaze (made by simply reducing
    75 ml chicken stock to 25 ml)
sea salt

To make the egg emulsion, cook the eggs for 9 minutes in a steamer at 100% steam. Blend the carrot, celeriac, vinegar and chicken glaze in a small blender. Add the eggs one by one, blending well between each addition, until the mixture forms a good thick consistency. Season with salt.

Trim the radishes, reserving the leaves, and cut them into quarters. Refresh the leaves in iced water and drain on paper towel.

Toss the potatoes in the melted butter and salt. Place the potatoes in a perforated tray and steam at 100% steam for 8 minutes. Add the peas and radishes and cook for a further 2 minutes. Remove the vegetables from the steamer and peel the potatoes.

Place the warm potatoes in a large bowl, mix through 1 tablespoon of the egg emulsion and season with salt. Arrange the potatoes on a plate with the peas and radishes, then scatter the dandelion leaves around the plate (if using).

Garnish with the radish leaves and serve.

Pickled onions

Makes 12

Pickling is one of the oldest methods of preservation in existence, and pickled vegetables play a big part in Czech cuisine. The recipe below is probably the easiest one in the entire book, and makes enough pickled onion for several recipes. Delicious with braised beef cheeks (see page 192), grilled fish, steak or a good salad.

200 g caster sugar
200 ml apple vinegar
200 ml water
200 ml beer
12 medium brown onions, peeled and
    cut in half

Combine the sugar, vinegar, water and beer in a large saucepan over medium heat and boil for 1 minute.

Place the onions in a large stainless steel bowl or a glass jar with a sealable lid, then pour the pickling liquid over the top. Refrigerate for at least 12 hours before serving. They will keep in the fridge for up to 2 weeks.

Wild honey doughnuts with poppy-seed sugar

Serves 4

I have really struggled to find a dessert that says 'Prague'. Fruit dumplings definitely fit the bill, but I feel they are not something you would cook at home unless you had eaten them before. They simply don't look as good as they taste. One sweet treat I did find in a lot of shops and on menus were doughnuts with fruit jam inside, which inspired the recipe below. You will need a Dutch pancake iron to make these doughnuts, and 2 piping bags, both of which are available at most kitchenware shops.

100 g butter, melted

Honey custard
4 egg yolks
15 g plain flour
15 g custard powder
10 g cornflour
¾ cup (180 ml) milk
50 g honey

Poppy-seed sugar
25 g poppy seeds
⅓ cup (75 g) sugar

Doughnut batter
125 g plain flour, sifted
5 eggs, separated
pinch of sea salt
½ cup (125 ml) cream
65 g butter, melted
25 g caster sugar

To make the honey custard, whisk together the egg yolks, flour, custard powder and cornflour in a bowl. Meanwhile, combine the milk and honey in small heavy-based saucepan and bring to the boil. Pour one third of the milk mixture into the egg mixture and mix until combined. Pour the egg mixture back into the hot milk in the pan, and cook over medium heat, whisking constantly, until thickened. Pour the custard into a tray, cover the surface closely with plastic film to prevent a skin forming and place in the fridge until cold. Transfer the custard to a piping bag and store in the fridge until needed.

For the poppy-seed sugar, grind the poppy seeds and sugar to a powder in a mortar and pestle. Place it in an airtight container.

To make the doughnut batter, place the flour, egg yolks, salt and cream in an electric mixer fitted with the whisk attachment and mix until combined. Add the melted butter and mix until it resembles a cake batter. Transfer to a mixing bowl. Clean the bowl, then return it to the mixer and fit with the whisk attachment. Add the egg whites and sugar and whisk to medium peaks.

Using a rubber spatula or spoon, fold one third of the egg whites into the cake batter (to loosen it), then fold in the remaining egg whites. Transfer the batter to a piping bag fitted with a 1 cm round nozzle and store in the fridge until you are ready to use it.

Preheat the oven on the conventional setting to 160°C.

Heat the Dutch pancake iron over an induction set on 6 or a gas burner over medium heat and grease with melted butter. Pipe batter into each mould of the iron. As the batter cooks on the outside, turn the doughnut with a wooden skewer by pressing down on the edge closest to the front. Continue this process, adding more batter to fill the gaps.

When three-quarters of the doughnut is complete, pipe some honey custard into the centre and cover with more batter. Place the iron in the oven for 1½ minutes or until the doughnuts are golden and cooked through. Remove.

While the doughnuts are still warm, roll them in the remaining melted butter, and coat in the poppy-seed sugar. Serve with the remaining honey custard.

Visitor tips

Hotels

Alchymist Grand Hotel and Spa ↓
Trziste 19, Prague 1, 110 00
☎ +420 257 286 011
alchymisthotel.com
The most over-the-top hotel in Prague (many have described it as looking like a rococo brothel), this place has lashings of gold and red, and drapes that would dazzle in any castle. Brilliantly designed and restored, with an Indonesian spa of your dreams downstairs and a muralled restaurant that transports you across the globe, as well as a precious jewel of a coffee-and-chocolate shop hidden away at the entrance, this is a magnificent hotel.

Aria Hotel
Trziste 368/9, 118 00
☎ +420 225 334 111
ariahotel.net
A glorious haven of calm and civilised hospitality. A musical theme runs throughout, from the treble-clef-shaped door key, to the music on the iPad in your room, to the CD library on the ground floor, where a specialist will find what you want to hear or see, recorded or live. A truly elegant and discreet hotel that will make any visit feel too short. If you can, get a room at the back overlooking the terraced gardens, but all rooms are superb.

The Augustine Hotel
Letenská 12/33, 118 00 Praha
☎ +420 266 112 233
theaugustine.com
A great Malá Strana hotel that still awaits its full day in the sun. The street it is on is a bit daunting with traffic and trams, but inside is a calm retreat. This could easily become the finest hotel in Prague.

Mandarin Oriental
Nebovidská 459/1, 118 00 Praha 1
☎ +420 233 088 888
mandarinoriental.com/prague
One of the grandest hotels on the Left Bank. In a privileged, quiet part of Malá Strana, this former monastery is now an elegant luxury hotel, though it's a little lacking in character.

Restaurants

Café Savoy
Vítězná 124/5, 150 00 Praha 5
☎ +420 257 311 562
cafesavoy.ambi.cz

Billed as a restaurant-pâtisserie-vinothèque, the Café Savoy was founded in 1893 and has been a Prague icon ever since. The design and atmosphere are superb.

Coda
Trziste 368/9, 118 00
☎ +420 225 334 761
codarestaurant.cz

Set in the luxurious surrounds of Aria Hotel; in fine weather, it moves up to the roof, a wonderful outdoor space with the peak of the hotel's roof rising up between diners. The food is light and modern, with a few re-interpreted Czech classics.

Hergetova Cihelná
Cihelná 2b, 118 00
☎ +420 296 826 103
kampagroup.com

A modern restaurant in an old building, beside the river and not far from Kampa Park (which is part of the same group). You can hardly see the river unless you sit outside, but the buzz inside from the young clientele is intoxicating. It serves some of the best modern food in Prague.

Kampa Park
Na Kampě 8b, 118 00
☎ +420 296 826 112
kampagroup.com

The most famous restaurant in Prague, nestled on the water's edge near the Charles Bridge. Insist on a table on the terrace and select one of the superb Czech wines. The food is modern and the quality variable, but often delicious.

SaSaZu
Bubenské nábřeží 306/13, 170 04
7-Holešovice
☎ +420 284 097 455
sasazu.com

Spearheading the boom in Asian cuisine in Prague, SaSaZu is the only restaurant I have ever heard of where one can get a massage after the main course. Set in the warehouse district, this bar-restaurant, with Vietnamese food by Israeli chef Shahaf Shabtay, is popular with locals.

Terasa U Zlaté Studně ↓
U Zlaté Studně 166/4, 118 00
☎ +420 257 533 322
terasauzlatestudne.cz

At the foot of Prague Castle, this restaurant boasts a terrace dining area with views over the red roofs of the old town to the Vltava River. Pavel Sapík is an inventive chef, with dishes such as flame-grilled sea scallops with rose champagne and strawberry carpaccio, along with Bohemian wine.

Santiago

Pride in its heritage and a rich mix of
cultural influences make this a great
food city, despite its poverty.

Framed by the Andes mountains, Santiago boasts a setting few cities can compete with. With 6.3 million people, this valley, an oasis in the arid landscape, is crammed with buildings new and old for as far as the eye can see. I wake up to a misty, eerie morning; what better way to start the day than to jog to the main city centre? The route takes me through the newly constructed park housing the impressive Stock Exchange building, heading downtown along the river past artworks and modern landscapes where the contrast between the new and the old could not be more distinct. The main square, Plaza Italian, also boasts wonderful parks and old architecture. I have run eight kilometres from the W Hotel, which is regarded as a central location, yet have only just reached the centre of the old town! Cafe Con Piernas is my second stop, considered the best coffee in town. I've also been recommended Cafe Cariba, Cafe Haiti and Cafe do Brasil.

Then it's on to the market, Vega Central de Santiago, open every day of the year until 2 p.m. It 'makes the city live' according to locals, and truly is the heartbeat of downtown. Its contrast to the 'uptown' of new buildings and Starbucks coffee shops is startling. To me Santiago is the flaking paint, rusted door frames and the people who inhabit them, their faces carved with the pressures of the daily grind yet still quick to smile. Life is as good as the last avocado you spread on your fresh bread. Poverty is an accepted part of the fabric of this society. It is a fact of life I have not had to confront before. When I mean poor I mean people who are lacking basic necessities. Just beyond the market walls, the desperation and fear is palpable. I feel more than a little intimidated, and deeply out of place. Santiago is quick to show off her riches, but she does not closet her darker truths. ➜

1   At a local herb farm, Sociedad Agricola Rosario.
2   The former National Congress Building, now open to the public.
3   A detail from the Stock Exchange building (also pictured opposite).

I enter the inner market with Mathieu Michel, a well-known local chef who Miele often use for their events, and it's as if the clouds have parted; the ambience could not be more different. We stop for coffee in the dirtiest, dingiest-looking cafe you could possibly imagine, yet it has a certain charm and allows you to look out on to the masses of people. Despite the noise, it feels serene. The owners of the cafe are a lovely couple in their fifties; we chat in a mash-up of Spanish and broken English. They are keen for me to enjoy the experience of their market.

They tell me to eat some *palta* (avocado) on fresh bread. This is the diet eight months of the year for most working-class Chileans. On weekends it is cold poached chicken, normally cooked at home using a pressure cooker. Everyone has a pressure cooker here, and white beans and lentils are part of the daily diet. A very important dish, *porotos con riendas*, is made with white beans cooked in meat stock and then spaghetti and pork sausage is added with whole carrots and a little bit of pumpkin, and a final glug of paprika oil as a garnish. They serve this to the hordes of market workers who pile in hour after hour during the early morning. It smells great.

The tastes of this city are practical; it is still learning how to showcase its cuisine. Big, high-calorie portions are still the order of the day. Produce that is easily farmed, such as chickens, are everywhere, and European influence is strong, especially in the array of vegetables. Culturally, Santiago lives in the shadows of Peru and Argentina. The biggest and most exciting part of the market is the Peruvian section. The smells, the colour, the sauces and the fantastic hole-in-the-wall restaurants really get the juices flowing.

Small restaurants are dotted throughout the market; if you walk into any of them in November, when the strawberry season is at its height, you will be offered freshly crushed strawberry juice. Peruvian influence is also felt in very subtle ways; sweet potatoes, red peppers, and several varieties of citrus including yuzu, spices and dried chillies. The market is a fantastic adventure. ➔

4–12 At the market. We stopped at this cafe for a breather before exploring the many vegetable stalls; it might look unprepossessing but it was actually the perfect place to stop and people-watch for a moment.

Time is slipping away; it is now 9 a.m. We head towards the airport to the closest agricultural region to the city, a rural area called Lumpa, where we are to visit a farm called Sociedad Agricola Rosario. The owner, Alonso, is excited to see us. He and his family specialise in local herbs, some native to the area, others introduced. Alonso and his family proudly show us around. All their irrigation is provided by melted snow running down from the Andes. I promise to send him some kale seeds, as he has never grown it before. I tell him it will be a huge hit at Vega market.

Mathieu then takes us to the 'university' area; no one has a clue as to why as there is no actual university there, but we are hungry and he knows a great little restaurant, La Mar, that produces simple dishes from local live lobster and oysters. Think classic 1970s Spanish decor. The extremely large tank holding the fish is very noticeable as you are escorted upstairs. It's all about grilled fish or lobsters with a great bottle of wine. The restaurant is known as a *picada*, meaning that the food is very honest and the restaurant is open all day. We are given a pisco sour on the house to start by the Peruvian barman. *Machas* is a local clam, and *locas* is a variety of abalone cooked in a pressure cooker, served with mayonnaise and onion and coriander salsa. King crab meat is picked, seasoned with salt and coriander and served with mayonnaise, pickles and melba toast. A great meal.

Thank god I decided to leave that last half of avocado stuffed with crab alone. Mathieu is not finished with me yet; our next stop is La Fuente Alemana, a local sandwich restaurant. He tells me that I cannot leave Santiago without coming here. ➜

13–15 At Sociedad Agricola Rosario, where honey and local herbs are produced.
16–19 At La Mar, where we are lavished with local seafood dishes.

The selection of sandwiches on offer is small but well chosen. The thinly sliced beef *Churrasco* is boiled for hours then seared on the steaming grill, as is the *Rumano*, a beef and pork patty seasoned with spice. The other fillings, *Salchichas* and *Gordas*, are hot-dog-like sausages, cut in half lengthways and packed with homemade tomato sauce, fresh tomatoes and a thick layer of avocado puree. *The Lomito*, La Fuente Alemana's best seller, is plain, thinly sliced pork beloved for its unadulterated meatiness and packed tightly with a classic Chilean garnish. They are seriously good sandwiches, and photos do not do justice to how big these monsters are. Desperately needing a nap on someone's couch, I psyche myself up for the event. Do I know this city yet? I am starting to. Am I loving it? You bet ya! It has that air of potential adventure in spades.

After the excitement of conducting my first-ever dinner during an earthquake (see the description on page 9) I am getting that fuzzy feeling that my journey is coming to an end. I will come back to Santiago; this city is a sleeper and an occasional shaker, and I have only touched the tip of the iceberg. ●

20–23 At La Fuente Alemana, where I did my best to fit in a sandwich on top of the huge seafood lunch we'd already eaten.

24   On the outskirts of the city, with the Andes mountains in the distance.

25   A pottery workshop where these beautiful handmade clay bowls, piggybanks and figurines are created and sold.

26   A friendly local, who was keen to tell us about the game he'd just won.

Prawn ceviche

Serves 2

Aguachile (literally 'chilli water') is a type of ceviche. It's so light and refreshing, making it the ideal dish to enjoy during summer in Chile, along with other staples such as fresh coriander and avocado.

20 large raw prawns, peeled and deveined, then cut in half lengthways
juice of 8 limes
juice of 2 oranges
2 jalapeno chillies, seeded and thinly sliced
good handful of coriander leaves, washed and chopped
¼ teaspoon cumin seeds, lightly toasted and crushed in a mortar and pestle
1 teaspoon sea salt
pinch of freshly ground black pepper
1 cucumber, cut in half lengthways and finely diced
1 red onion, peeled, cut in half and finely diced
snowpea tendrils, to garnish
8 iceberg lettuce cups

Place the prawns in a ceramic dish and lay them out flat. Squeeze over the lime juice and leave to marinate in the fridge for 1 hour.

Remove two-thirds of the juice from the prawns and pour it into a blender or food processor. Keep the remaining juice in the dish with the prawns and return to the fridge.

Add the orange juice, chilli, coriander and cumin to the lime juice and blend until smooth. Season with salt and pepper.

Drain the remaining lime juice from the prawns and discard it. Arrange the prawns flat on individual plates or a large platter and spoon the sauce over the top. Garnish with a fine dice of cucumber and red onion, and a few snowpea tendrils, and serve with iceberg lettuce leaves to wrap.

Pastel de choclo –
the Chilean meat pie

Serves 6

Served in many homes, I found this dish really quite addictive, especially when offered with a mixture of chopped pickled gherkins, capers, coriander and jalapenos, with a simple beef tomato salad on the side. A snack-sized version is similar to a Mexican tamale, where a corn husk encases the corn and mince filling, which is then tied and steamed, and served with pickles on the side.

1 tablespoon olive oil or chicken,
    pork or beef fat
800 g beef mince
200 g pork mince
4 medium brown onions, peeled, cut in half
    and roughly chopped
2 teaspoons cumin seeds, lightly toasted
    and crushed in a mortar and pestle
2 tablespoons chopped basil
1/3 cup (50 g) raisins
1/3 cup (40 g) black pitted local olives
3 hard-boiled eggs, peeled and chopped
sea salt and freshly ground black pepper
2 teaspoons caster sugar
3 cups (600 g) corn kernels (fresh or frozen),
    steamed for 10 minutes or until soft
60 g cultured butter, diced
1 cup (250 ml) chicken stock
1 tablespoon polenta or cornmeal
1 tablespoon coarse breadcrumbs
    or panko crumbs

Heat the olive oil or fat in a heavy casserole dish over medium heat and cook the mince until it is finely broken up and thoroughly cooked. Remove and place in a colander over a bowl to allow the meat to drain off all excess fat. Discard the fat. Return the dish to medium heat and cook the onion until softened and slightly golden, then add the ground cumin.

Put the drained meat back in the dish and cook for 1 minute. Add the basil, raisins, olives and chopped egg and stir into the mince. Season generously with salt, pepper and sugar, and remove from the heat.

Preheat the oven on the conventional setting to 180°C.

Place the corn kernels, butter and half the stock in a food processor or blender and process until smooth. Add the remaining stock gradually until the mixture reaches the consistency of a thick paste – you may not need all the stock. Season well with salt and pepper. Spoon the puree over the meat mixture, smooth the top and sprinkle over the polenta or cornmeal and breadcrumbs to form a crust. Bake for 10–12 minutes or until golden.

Leche asada

Serves 8

This is like a Chilean version of creme caramel, only larger, served with grilled mandarins or oranges on the side. I found a great cake stall in the Vega market that served a spectacularly light, sweet and bitter version, so I asked for the recipe. I have made a small variation by adding pisco to the caramel, which imparts a subtly aromatic flavour. Note: when using a steamer, no bain marie is required.

cooking oil spray
450 ml water
500 g caster sugar
¼ cup (60 ml) good-quality pisco liqueur
2 cups (500 ml) cream
2 cups (500 ml) full-cream milk
10 egg yolks
4 mandarins, cut into 6–8 wedges each
viola flowers, to garnish (optional)

Preheat the steamer to 88°C.

Lightly spray 8 × 1 cup (250 ml) ramekins with cooking spray.

Combine the water and 300 g caster sugar in a medium heavy-based saucepan over an induction set on 8 and boil until a golden caramel forms. Remove from the heat and pour two-thirds of the caramel into the ramekins.

Place the remaining caramel back on the stove over an induction set on 6 and bring to the boil. Add the pisco and boil for 2 minutes, then fold in 200 ml cream. While it is still hot, pour the caramel into the ramekins to a depth of 2 cm.

Place the milk, egg yolks, remaining cream and remaining sugar in a large bowl and mix with a stick blender or a hand-held mixer until smooth. Pour over the set caramel in the ramekins, then place them in the steamer and cook for 30 minutes or until set. Remove and set aside to cool for at least an hour before serving.

Briefly heat a small, sharp pointy knife in hot water, then gently run the knife around the inside of each ramekin. Then gently tip the ramekin upside-down and turn out the puddings into serving dishes.

Preheat a chargrill and grill the mandarin segments on both sides until caramelised. Arrange over the puddings, garnish with viola flowers (if using) and serve.

Visitor tips

Hotels

Noi Vitacura Hotel ↓
Avenue Nueva Costanera 3736, Vitacura
☎ **+56 2941 8000**
noivitacure.cl
Great boutique hotel in the new part of
the city, featuring rooftop bar and pool.
Rooms are modern with restrained charm
throughout the design. I prefer this place
to the W Hotel but it may not suit all
international travellers or those with high
expectations.

W Hotel
Isidora Goyenechea 3000,
Los Condes 7550653
☎ **+56 2 2770 0000**
starwoodhotels.com
Positioned in the new uptown part of
the city (a little soulless compared to
downtown). A well-appointed hotel
with very good staff and a great bar and
restaurants. It does lose the Santiago feel
with its modern decor but for the young,
energetic traveller it has its place.

Restaurants

Borago Restaurant
Avenida Nueva Costanera 3467, Vitacura
☎ **+56 2 953 8893**
borago.cl
Rodolfo Guzman is the most famous chef to
celebrate Chilean food. He forages through
the Andes looking for indigenous herbs
and flowers to add to his ideas. Be warned,
this is the most expensive restaurant in
Santiago, at approximately AUD$100 per
person for his degustation menu.

El Hoyo
Calle San Vicente 363, Santiago,
Región Metropolitana
☎ **+56 2 689 0339**
elhoyo.cl
A very popular typical Chilean restaurant
that a lot of locals rave about.

Osaka Restaurant @ W Hotel
Isidora Goyenechea 3000, Las Condes,
West Santiago
☎ **+56 2 770 0000**
starwoodhotels.com/whotels/
property/dining
Nikai cuisine is a fusion between Peruvian
and Japanese, with great food in a modern
setting. Well worth the booking. Some of
the best seafood you will eat anywhere.
Ask for a unique shellfish called *picoroco*,
'the stone of the sea', an essential Chilean
seafood. Normally cooked over hot coals
or eaten raw.

La Mar Restaurant ↓
Nueva Costanera 4076, Vitacura
☎ **+56 2 206 7839**
lamarcebicheria.cl
Delicious local seafood and pisco sours are
the specialties here.

Seattle

A centre of industry and famous as the
'birthplace of grunge', Seattle also
has a thriving food and coffee scene.

We all know Seattle is famous for Boeing, Amazon and Microsoft; some may also know that Starbucks originated here, at the Pike Place Market. Seattle is also a hub for independent coffee roasters and baristas, chocolatiers, craft beer makers and breweries, and Columbia Valley Wines, as well as being home to seven different species of wild salmon, as well as wild haddock and the Dungeness crab. To my delight, it is also the epicentre of sustainability research and development in America. In fact, that is the reason the president of Miele USA, Nick Ord, asked me to come over to Seattle. Nick, a real new-age foodie, is determined to help Seattle become better known for its great food culture. I have the next thirty hours to discover it. Straight off the plane, I am immediately swept up at the airport by the local team. There is no time to waste; they are eager to get me to the Pike Place Markets. I dump my bags at the Edgewater Hotel and off we go.

We stop off at the cheesecake shop at the markets, The Confectional, where Paul Verano makes an eight-ounce cup of his grandmother's hot chocolate flavoured with clove and cinnamon for a bargain $4.50, and have a slice of his famous baked raspberry and white chocolate cheesecake. He was over the moon when I chatted to him, as he had just picked up the contract to supply Microsoft. From here, we stroll along to cheese-maker Beecher's, famous for its mac 'n' cheese. Most of Kurt Beecher's cheeses are actually made on site. ➔

1   Elliot Bay and Seattle Harbour.
2–3   The home of Starbucks, Seattle also has plenty of independent coffee roasters and baristas.
4   Food prep at Chan, one of Seattle's most exciting Korean restaurants.
5   Cheesecakes being made at The Confectional.

Modernist Cuisine

Without doubt the most famous cookbook to come out of America in the modern era is the five-volume *Modernist Cuisine*, a well-known publication in the chef world. When you listen to Chris, a chef and entrepreneur of *Modernist Cuisine*, talk about the years spent on research and development for the book, all sponsored by Microsoft, you realise how reasonable the $500 price tag is. In fact, the authors have celebrated recently reaching the $35 million sales mark. They have formed a website called www.chefssteps.com to share tips and teach techniques, and are nearly at the stage of charging for courses on their website. They assist home cooks and chefs with everything from macarons to creating the perfect roast pork or even a gluten-free carrot cake. Look this one up on the website; 'amazing' doesn't do it justice.

Time for a quick sandwich break, so we head over past the original Starbucks, where there are queues out the door, twenty deep! We are going to the Rub with Love Shack, which is a sandwich shop that sells rubs and other small kitchen ingredients, owned by well-known chef Tom Douglas, the local food 'sultan of Seattle', so to speak. He owns fourteen restaurants, all within walking distance of each other – that is his stipulation, that he has to be able to walk between them all each day. The sandwiches are excellent value for money. I pick up a local personal food tour guide, Mark Boeker, who can be booked for all sorts of foodie tours around the city. →

6　I was amazed to see a queue outside Starbucks, but this is the first branch ever opened, in its city of origin.

7　At BB Ranch Butchers, enjoying a moment of local rye appreciation with William von Schneidau, aka Bill the Butcher.

8　One of the stalls at Pike Place Markets.

9　Ba Bar, one of Eric Banh's establishments, specialising in Vietnamese street food and craft cocktails.

We stop off at the restaurant Chan to meet the chef and owner Park Heong Soon, who uses mostly local produce to create his modern Korean cuisine. Then, walking left out of Park's door, we have all of one minute's walk to BB Ranch Butchers. William von Schneidau, the butcher and owner, is a professional presenter and showman who only sources products from small independent farmers. Currently he is designing a method for onsite abattoirs. And then it's time to leave Pike Place; I could rave on for several pages about the market here but simply put, it's the heartbeat of Seattle.

We head towards the Capitol Hill area with Eric Banh, who came to the US as a young refugee from Vietnam. He was destined to be an accountant until he started to pay his way through senior high school in kitchens. His father didn't speak to him for a month after he broke the news that he loved the industry so much he wanted to stay put and drop out of college. Since then he has never looked back. He has two restaurants in Seattle; he tells me to eat at Ba Bar. The grey sky starts to darken.

Jetlag is starting to set in, six hours off the flight, so I suggest a quick whisky cocktail. My Irish uncles taught me to handle everything from jetlag to the flu this way – whisky! We drop in on two bars we were recommended: Tavern Law and The Old Sage on Capitol Hill, where a large part of the music culture scene was born. The barman, Michael, was a little grumpy to start – he asked me for ID! I told him my thoughts on that policy in no uncertain terms; rather than throwing me out, he lightened up and convinced me to try a gin saffron sour topped with a tincture, which I had never heard of before. It is a type of single flavoured bitters. Also try the coffee-based cocktail called the Treaty of Paris; it really hits the spot. The bar also does great little French-inspired dishes to share, such as terrines and salads. ➜

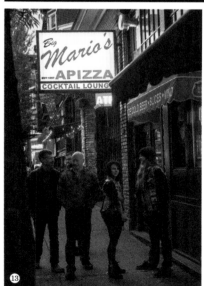

10–12 Inside Ba Bar.
13 Outside Big Mario's Pizza and Cocktail Lounge.
14 At the City Fish Market.

Michael tells me all about the local spirit, apple jack brandy, a raw version of calvados that has become part of American food and beverage culture; most say it is fabulous to cook with, especially with the local wild salmon. Tavern Law also has a 'secret' little speakeasy bar, opened to those in the know five nights a week. Reservations can be made; no menu, just cocktails made to your liking. It captures some of the atmosphere of America in the 1920s during prohibition. Michael jokes it was actually easier to serve liquor back then, as the current laws in Seattle are complicated and can make it hard to run a good bar.

The Old Sage next door does some seriously great food. I highly recommend this for a dinner destination. I organise to meet the owner, Brian McCracken, along with Jason Franey, head chef of Canalis restaurant, for a quick drink. Franey is regarded as Seattle's finest chef and I'm not disappointed by his passion and determination to make a name for himself. He loves the produce that surrounds Seattle; all he needs is time and more food tourists to try out the seventy-year-old restaurant, which astonishingly has only ever employed five head chefs in its entire history. In the meantime, he is working on using fish species that are not currently popular, such as skate. ➜

15–17 At Tavern Law, where I try apple jack brandy, a local spirit.

Live music

Seattle is famous for its music scene; many well-known bands and musicians became famous after playing at Capitol Hill, although the number of music venues there is shrinking. Jimi Hendrix, Nirvana and Pearl Jam all got their start here. Moe's is one of the dwindling number of music venues left on Capitol Hill. Let's hope someone with skill and knowledge reinvents these venues for the next generation of bands to come.

After a great night's sleep, I wake up to the sound of sea birds out my window. Coffee is in order. After a one-mile walk uphill along Pike, I'm feeling a little lightheaded and go looking for a good cup of coffee. Everyone I meet in Seattle has told me to go to Caffe Vita, and indeed the coffee is just what I need. It's single origin, from the Congo, served as a pour-over in filter paper. I talk to Bob Prince, one of the partners in Vita. He says the vivid Seattle coffee scene started with the original Starbucks at Pike Place Market in 1983, which paved the way for other small roasters to set up. Bob and his team now roast 2 tonnes of beans a day and run fourteen cafes. The feel is very similar to Melbourne: simple, friendly, unimposing and filled with the aroma of fresh roasted coffee.

Seattle was a litmus test for me. Relatively speaking, it is a young city – younger than Melbourne – yet it has a well-defined food culture. People here are in love with the fact you can get a reservation at any great restaurant at a moment's notice. It gives me hope for my home town! ●

18–20 Caffe Vita, a local independent coffee roaster. Two tonnes of coffee beans go through this roasting machine every day.

Slow-cooked wild salmon with apple and dungeness crab

Serves 4

Spending time in Seattle has reinforced my belief that salmon farming is wrong for so many reasons. Up to 8 species of salmon are sold in the markets around Seattle, all wild and all incredibly different in colour and texture, depending on the diet and behaviour of the species. Some larger species like king salmon have a live-fish-based diet, resulting in a pale flesh, while some of the smaller species (don't be deceived – they still weigh at least 4 kilograms!) are bright red due to a diet of krill and small shrimps. The carotene in the crustaceans causes the flesh to turn this intense colour.

In most farms salmon are bred in small pens, often crammed together in environments they don't normally inhabit, and fed on dried pellets filled with antibiotics, reconstituted wild ocean by-catch, poultry bones and food colour. Starting to get the picture? Seattle is the place to come and try the real stuff. To top it all off, it is also the home of the legendary dungeness crab.

1 tablespoon olive oil
sea salt
4 × 80 g salmon fillets, skin and bones removed
4 tablespoons cooked and picked dungeness
   crab meat
1 teaspoon Japanese mayonnaise
grated zest and juice of ¼ lemon, or to taste
1 granny smith apple, cut into quarters
   and thinly sliced
handful of watercress sprigs
4 pickled baby onions (see page 195),
   cut in half
1 tablespoon quince or apple vinegar
2 tablespoons pumpkin seed oil

Preheat the oven to 85°C on the combi steam setting with 30% moisture. Line a baking tray with baking paper.

Rub the olive oil and 1 teaspoon salt all over the salmon pieces, then place on the prepared tray and bake for 16 minutes. When the timer goes off, leave the door closed and don't open it until you are ready to serve.

Mix the crab meat with the mayonnaise, and season to taste with lemon zest, lemon juice and salt.

Spoon the crab meat evenly onto each plate, add the salmon and garnish each serve with 3 slices of apple, a few sprigs of watercress and 2 pickled onion halves. Whisk together the vinegar and pumpkin seed oil and drizzle over the top.

The 'shroom burger'

Serves 4

Mushrooms are a big part of the local food culture in Seattle, especially in the late autumn, and burgers are also taken extremely seriously. Add to this the fact that gluten-free, low-carb diets are now the norm in many households and it's clear why the 'shroom burger' is so popular. They are best served simply with a good side salad and some homemade fries (in my opinion, yukon gold potatoes work best for these). The braised beef patty can be replaced with whatever you choose – for the full vegetarian option, try roasted vegetable slices.

**8 large portabello mushrooms,
    stems removed**
sea salt
olive oil, for drizzling
**10–12 rashers streaky bacon, baked
    until crispy**
100 g feta, crumbled
¼ Chinese cabbage, well washed and torn

Tomato chutney
1 tablespoon olive oil
**1 small red onion, cut in half, peeled
    and finely diced**
2 cloves garlic, finely chopped
1 long red chilli, seeded and finely chopped
1 tablespoon mustard seeds
200 g canned tomatoes
4 tomatoes, roughly chopped
2 teaspoons brown sugar, or to taste
1 tablespoon apple vinegar, or to taste
sea salt

Braised beef patties
400 g beef shin
1.2 litres chicken stock
1 tablespoon finely chopped golden shallot
1 tablespoon finely chopped flat-leaf parsley
1 teaspoon finely grated lemon zest
sea salt
1 tablespoon olive oil

To braise the meat for the patties, preheat the oven on the conventional setting to 180°C. Put the beef in a casserole dish with the stock (the stock should be just covering the meat), cover with a lid or foil, then braise gently in the oven for 4 hours. Take it out and check that the beef is tender enough to pull apart. Strain the stock into a saucepan and reduce over medium heat for 30 minutes or until it is thick enough to coat the back of a spoon. Reserve the reduced stock for later.

While the stock is reducing, return the beef to the casserole dish and let it cool uncovered on the bench. When cool, use your hands to shred the beef into rough 1 cm pieces.

To make the tomato chutney, heat the olive oil in a small saucepan over an induction set on 6 or a gas burner over medium heat, add the onion, garlic, chilli and mustard seeds and cook until the onion is transparent. Add the remaining ingredients and bring to the boil, then reduce the heat and simmer for 30 minutes. Season to taste with salt and possibly more vinegar and sugar. Set aside until ready to serve.

Meanwhile, to make the patties, line a shallow baking tin (about 3 cm deep) with baking paper. Combine the shredded beef, shallot, parsley, lemon zest and ½ cup (125 ml) of the reduced braising stock in a bowl and season to taste with salt. Press the meat into the prepared tin, to a thickness of about 2 cm, and cover with baking paper. Allow to set in the fridge for 1 hour.

Preheat the oven on intensive bake to 220°C and line a baking tray with baking paper.

Season the mushrooms with salt, place them on the prepared tray, bottoms up, and drizzle liberally with olive oil. Place an oven rack over the top of the mushrooms and bake for 15 minutes or until cooked. Cover and rest until you are ready to serve.

While the mushrooms are cooking, remove the patty tray from the fridge, carefully turn out the pressed meat and cut into 4 even 6 cm squares (or rounds if preferred). Heat the olive oil in a large heavy-based frying pan over an induction set on 8 or a gas burner over medium–high heat and add some salt to the pan. When hot, add the patties and cook on each side for 2 minutes or until they are a dark brown colour and have formed a crust. Remove from the pan and rest on paper towel.

To assemble the burgers, place the meat patties on 4 of the mushrooms, then add the bacon, crumbled feta and some torn cabbage leaves. Season with salt, then place the remaining mushrooms on top and press firmly. Serve with tomato chutney to the side.

Eskimo Joe ice-cream sandwich with salted caramel sauce

Makes 8

Eskimo Joes and Monaco bars were my favourite ice-creams when I was growing up. Combine that with how big the Miele master cool freezers are in America, and it wasn't much of a leap to make a parfait to fill this giant freezer with. Ice-cream, dense chocolate biscuit and salted caramel fit the profile for a Seattle-type dessert, especially at many of the great diners and burger bars. Did I mention Dick's Burgers?!

125 g butter
60 g icing sugar
1 cup (150 g) flour
¼ cup (30 g) almond meal
40 g cocoa powder
1 egg yolk
2 teaspoons water

Vanilla parfait
10 egg yolks
250 g caster sugar
1 tablespoon pure vanilla extract
600 ml cream, lightly whipped to a 'ribbon' consistency

Salted caramel sauce
240 g caster sugar
150 ml water, plus extra if needed
125 g cultured butter, at room temperature, cut into cubes
2 teaspoons sea salt

To make the parfait, line a 30 cm × 20 cm baking tin with baking paper. Fill a medium saucepan two-thirds full of water and simmer over an induction set on 6. Place a large stainless steel bowl over the saucepan, add the egg yolks and sugar and whisk vigorously until they are light, fluffy and pale in colour. Whisk in the vanilla extract. Remove the bowl from the heat and carefully fold in the cream until fully incorporated. Pour into the prepared baking tin, ensuring the parfait is at least 3 cm thick. Place the tray in the freezer and allow to set for at least 4 hours at minus 16°C.

Preheat the oven on intensive bake to 160°C.

Place the butter and icing sugar in an electric mixer fitted with the whisk attachment and whisk on high speed until the mixture has turned creamy white. Reduce the speed to medium and add the flour, almond meal and cocoa powder. Once fully incorporated, add the egg yolk and water to form a very basic dough.

Turn out the dough onto a clean work surface and gently roll out to a 5 mm thickness. Using a sharp knife, cut the dough into 8 cm × 4 cm rectangles and place on a non-stick tray (you will need 16 rectangles all up). Bake for 6 minutes, then set aside to cool completely on the tray.

To make caramel sauce, place the sugar and water in a medium saucepan over an induction set on 8 and boil until a golden colour starts to form. Add the butter and boil for 5 minutes. If the butter separates from the caramel, add 1 tablespoon cold water and boil again. Stir in the salt, them pour the sauce into bottle or jug and keep warm.

To assemble, remove the parfait from the freezer and cover with a layer of baking paper. Turn the tray upside down onto a board and peel off the paper from the bottom. Using a knife dipped in hot water cut the parfait into 8 rectangles, using one of the biscuits as template.

Sandwich each rectangle of parfait between 2 biscuits, then pour over some caramel sauce and serve immediately.

Visitor tips

Bars

The Old Sage
1410 12th Ave, 98122
☎ +1 206 557 7430
theoldsageseattle.com
Next door to Tavern Law, this is the place
to come for a special dinner made from
local produce.

Tavern Law ↓
1406 12th Ave, 98122
☎ +1 206 322 9734
tavernlaw.com
Unusual cocktails – try one that uses the
local spirit, apple jack – and great bar food.

Cafes, patisseries and casual eateries

Ba Bar →
550 12th Ave
☎ +1 206 328 2030
babarseattle.com
This small eatery, open for twenty
hours on most days, is a great spot for an
authentic bowl of pho or a 'Pate Chaud' –
a homemade puff pastry in the shape of
a vol au vent, filled with spiced chicken
mince and topped with a delicately cooked
fried egg oozing through the mince.
I thought of it as a Seattle meat pie.

Caffe Vita
1005 E Pike St, 98122
☎ +1 206 709 4440
caffevita.com
The best coffee in the home of coffee.
Single-origin coffee in a friendly,
relaxed atmosphere.

Rub with Love Shack
rubwithloveshack.com
2010 Western Ave, 98121
☎ +1 206 436 0390
A great little sandwich shop near
the markets.

Hotels

Edgewater Hotel
2411 Alaskan Way, Seattle, 98121
☎ +1 206 728 7000
edgewaterhotel.com
Ask for the Beatles suite if you book here.
There's a view over the bay, which is
renowned for the calm, glass-like water.
The hotel is in a great location, well-priced,
and it has a nice feel to it. I can only
imagine how beautiful my room would be
in the middle of summer with the windows
opening up on to the water.

Markets

Pike Place Market
85 Pike St, 98101
☎ +1 206 682 7453
pikeplacemarket.org
Opened over 120 years ago, this is literally
the foodie centre of town. Locals flock here
on weekends for supplies and a bite to eat.

Restaurants

Chan
86 Pine St, 98101
☎ +1 206 443 5443
chanseattle.com
This intimate 37-seater is the creation of
chef and owner Park Heong Soon. Born
and raised in Korea, he uses regional
ingredients with a slight French influence;
think braised shrimp and tofu roll or pork
belly flat bread (like a Korean soft-shell
taco). It's really worth the visit. Ninety-five
per cent of Park's produce is local, a passion
I can well understand, as he is so close to
the excellent market.

Restaurant Local 360 Miles
2234 1st Ave, 98121
☎ +1 206 441 9360
local360.org
This is the restaurant of the future.
Nothing, and I mean nothing, is served at
this restaurant that comes from outside
a radius of 360 miles. I think that's a sign of
how far advanced and confident the Seattle
food scene really is.

Shanghai

Street food, dumplings and noodles should be your first priority in this 'New York of the Far East'.

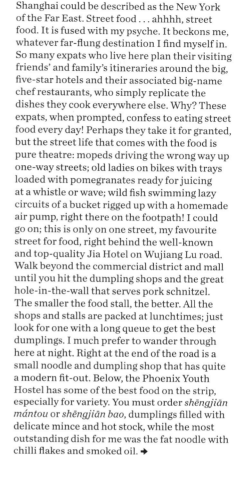

Shanghai could be described as the New York of the Far East. Street food . . . ahhhh, street food. It is fused with my psyche. It beckons me, whatever far-flung destination I find myself in. So many expats who live here plan their visiting friends' and family's itineraries around the big, five-star hotels and their associated big-name chef restaurants, who simply replicate the dishes they cook everywhere else. Why? These expats, when prompted, confess to eating street food every day! Perhaps they take it for granted, but the street life that comes with the food is pure theatre: mopeds driving the wrong way up one-way streets; old ladies on bikes with trays loaded with pomegranates ready for juicing at a whistle or wave; wild fish swimming lazy circuits of a bucket rigged up with a homemade air pump, right there on the footpath! I could go on; this is only on one street, my favourite street for food, right behind the well-known and top-quality Jia Hotel on Wujiang Lu road. Walk beyond the commercial district and mall until you hit the dumpling shops and the great hole-in-the-wall that serves pork schnitzel. The smaller the food stall, the better. All the shops and stalls are packed at lunchtimes; just look for one with a long queue to get the best dumplings. I much prefer to wander through here at night. Right at the end of the road is a small noodle and dumpling shop that has quite a modern fit-out. Below, the Phoenix Youth Hostel has some of the best food on the strip, especially for variety. You must order *shēngjiān mántou* or *shēngjiān bao*, dumplings filled with delicate mince and hot stock, while the most outstanding dish for me was the fat noodle with chilli flakes and smoked oil. ➜

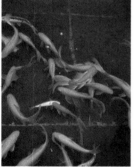

1   This amazing-looking building is the Oriental Pearl Radio and TV Tower.
2   Booths at the Shanghai Hyatt.
3–5 Dumplings of all kinds are a specialty of the thriving street food culture in this city.

Many of the food stalls appear practically Italian. Cured pork and sausage shops, fresh vegetable stalls with all the vegetables we know, plus dozens we don't. Pasta, or noodles as we call them here, spaghetti, penne, tagliatelle and more. I imagine that despite the towering skyscrapers, the streets are still very similar to the way they were when Marco Polo travelled through these lands, if not even the same. No one who lives on these streets takes their meal for granted. I find it sad that many expats have such a lack of respect for street food; they see it as too crowded, too noisy, too dirty. A missed opportunity to eat history in my opinion. Even in the markets, late in the day, it is worth wandering through to see whole families from grandma to grandchild all sitting together on makeshift crates and tables enjoying a spread of homemade dishes from tofu hotpots to braised pork with eggplant.

The Chinese description of Shanghainese food as sweet and oily does not do it justice. An oily texture is much needed to carry its intense and complex flavours. ●

6–18 In and around the markets and dumpling shops of the commercial district.
19 The concept of luck is a huge part of Chinese culture, and there's a roaring trade in good luck charms such as these.
20 Lantern-lit archways such as these give the city a distinctly Asian character.
21 The view from the hotel room.
22–25 Around the historic city of Ningbo, where we were taken to see a traditional Chinese opera.
26 A cocktail at M Glamour Bar.

Sheng jian bao

Makes 16

I was amazed to find out that most avid home cooks will make these from time to time. We just had to give it a go. Basically they are simple, juicy pork buns wrapped in bread dough, then fried on a flat, oil-slicked griddle until the bottoms are crispy. You will find them being sold for breakfast on most street corners. They are utterly irresistible – just try walking past.

¼ cup (60 ml) vegetable oil
1 tablespoon finely sliced ginger,
    cut into thin strips
2 tablespoons rice wine vinegar

Pork filling
280 g fatty pork mince
2 cloves garlic, minced
2 teaspoons minced ginger
3 spring onions, finely chopped
pinch of freshly ground white pepper
1½ tablespoons white sugar
½ teaspoon sea salt
2 teaspoons light soy sauce
2 tablespoons rice wine vinegar
1 teaspoon sesame oil

Dough
200 ml lukewarm water
1½ teaspoons instant dried yeast
2½ cups (375 g) plain flour

To make the pork filling, place all the ingredients in a bowl and mix well. Cover and leave in the fridge for 1 hour to allow the flavours to develop.

To make the dough, combine the water and yeast in a large stainless steel bowl. Add the flour, then turn out onto a bench and knead into a smooth dough. Return to the bowl and cover with a damp, clean tea towel. Leave to prove in a warm place for 30 minutes or until doubled in size.

Preheat the steamer to 100°C.

On a clean surface, knock back the dough to its original size. Cut it in half, then roll each portion into a sausage shape about 8 cm in diameter. Cut each portion into 8 pieces and roll into flat rounds about 10 cm in diameter. Place a tablespoon of the pork mixture in the centre of each round, then fold the dough in half and pinch the ends together. Arrange in a single layer in a steamer tray, then place in the steamer for 15 minutes. Remove and rest on a tray.

Heat a large flat chargrill pan or heavy frying pan over high heat and add the vegetable oil. Once the pan is smoking, add the dumplings, bottom-side down, and fry until crisp and dark golden.

Mix together the ginger and rice wine vinegar and serve with the dumplings as a dipping sauce.

Mapo doufu

Serves 4

Mapo doufu is one of those dishes that falls into the category of 'Mum has the best recipe' amongst the Shanghainese. No one can resist a bowl of what I am absolutely convinced is the true inspiration for spaghetti bolognese.

2½ tablespoons vegetable oil
3 cloves garlic, finely chopped
1 tablespoon finely chopped ginger
2 teaspoons Sichuan peppercorns,
    lightly crushed
200 g fatty beef mince (preferably wagyu)
2 tablespoons fermented chilli bean paste
2 tablespoons Chinese cooking wine
1 tablespoon light soy sauce
1 cup (250 ml) chicken stock
2 tablespoons chilli oil
2 tablespoons sesame oil
1 tablespoon cornflour
2 tablespoons cold water
400 g silken tofu, strained and
    cut into 2–3 cm cubes
1 tablespoon finely chopped garlic chives
steamed rice, to serve

Combine the vegetable oil, garlic, ginger, peppercorns and mince in a bowl, then set aside for 15–20 minutes to allow the flavours to develop. Fry the mixture in a hot wok over a wok induction set on 7 or a gas burner over medium heat for 5–6 minutes or until the mince is cooked through, breaking up any lumps as you go.

Add the paste, wine, soy sauce, stock, chilli oil and sesame oil, then taste and adjust the seasoning as needed. Reduce the heat to induction set on 5 or low heat on a gas burner and simmer for 5 minutes.

Blend the cornflour and water until smooth, then stir into the mixture in the wok until thickened. Just before serving, carefully fold in the tofu. Garnish with garlic chives and serve with steamed rice.

Egg tarts

Makes 16 small tarts

Melbourne is famed for its Portuguese tarts.
In Shanghai, somewhere along the way a similar
recipe has made its way to the doorstep of most
eating houses. They have the same freshly baked
texture, the addictive sweet/salty combination of
the silky custard, and the irresistible crumbling
pastry. I'm convinced these tarts actually *lower*
my cholesterol purely from the happiness they
bring me.

5 egg yolks, lightly beaten
90 g caster sugar
15 g plain flour
¾ cup (180 ml) cream
140 ml milk
20 g sweetened condensed milk
generous pinch of sea salt

Pastry
125 g butter
20 g icing sugar
1 egg, lightly beaten
1½ cups (225 g) plain flour
2 pinches of sea salt

To make the pastry, place the butter and icing
sugar in an electric mixer fitted with the whisk
attachment and beat until very pale. Reduce the
speed to low and add the beaten egg in 3 batches.
Add the flour in 2 batches and the salt, then stop the
mixer and gently form the dough into a ball. Roll it
out to a thickness of 2.5 cm, then place it on a tray,
cover with plastic film or a tea towel and rest in the
fridge for 30 minutes.

Preheat the oven on intensive bake to 180°C.

Remove the dough from the fridge and
divide it into 16 even pieces. Roll out each piece
on a floured, cold bench to a thickness of 5 mm
and gently press into 16 small fluted tart cases,
allowing the excess to drape over the sides.

Bake the pastry cases for 4 minutes then, using
another baking case of the same size, press the
dough down as it will have puffed up during baking.
Return the cases to the oven for another 4 minutes.
They won't be fully cooked at this stage, but this
is fine as they will go back in the oven again later.
Remove the second tray and set aside to cool while
you make the filling.

Reduce the oven temperature to 130°C.

Combine the egg yolks, sugar, flour, cream,
milk, condensed milk and salt in a large bowl and
whisk until there are no lumps. Pour the custard
evenly into the tart cases, filling them right to the
top. Bake for 20 minutes. Remove and rest for
5 minutes, then (if you like) trim the excess pastry
from the sides of the cases. Carefully remove the
tarts from the tins and serve while still warm –
ideally with a pot of jasmine tea.

Visitor tips

Bars

Sir Elly's Bar at The Peninsula
32 Zhongshan East 1st Rd, Huangpu
200002
☎ +86 21 2327 2888 ext. 6756
peninsula.com/shanghai
This bar has a rooftop deck looking out
over the Huangpu River to the skyline
dominated by the new Shanghai Tower,
and from here you can truly see what a
diverse, exciting city Shanghai is. Watch
the old sailing boats now fitted with super-
sized LED screens, boasting old films and
karaoke, floating downstream packed
with locals enjoying the high life.

Hotels

The Long Bar at the Puli Spa and Hotel
Jing'an, 1 Changde Rd
☎ +86 21 3203 9999
thepuli.com/en/dining-and-
entertainment/long-bar/
Very sexy hotel and bar.

Park Hyatt Shanghai
100 Century Avenue, Pudong, 200120
☎ +86 21 6888 1234
shanghai.park.hyatt.com
For its view, consistent high-quality
service, and location, this is one of my
favourites in this city.

The Peninsula
32 Zhongshan East 1st Rd, Huangpu
200002
☎ +86 21 2327 2888
peninsula.com/shanghai
If you're staying on the other side of the
river, the Peninsula has the complete
luxury package.

Nightclubs

Unico
2F, No.3 Zhong Shan Dong Yi Road
☎ +86 21 5308 5399
unico.cn.com
Not your traditional nightclub of dark
smoky spaces with banging music. Food
is the centre of attention here, with
well-known chef of Mirazur fame, Mauro
Colgreco, working the plates. Go from
small tapas nibbles to wood-grilled fish
and steaks, influenced by Colgreco's
Argentinean homeland.

Out-of-town escape

Ningbo
travelchinaguide.com/cityguides/
zhejiang/ningbo/transportation
Three hours' drive south of Shanghai is
a small, historic town called Ningbo. When
I say small, it does have a population of four
million – but you won't notice a soul when
staying at the Park Hyatt resort on Lake
Ningbo, set amongst 800-year-old temples
with not a westerner in sight.

Restaurants

A DA Shallot pancake
Maoming Road, Lane 159, No 2 at the
back door, near Nanchang Road
Best onion pancake in Shanghai.

Nanxiang Mantou (Yu Gardens)
85 Yuyuan Lu
☎ +86 21 6355 4206
Open from 7:30 a.m. until 9 p.m. in the
historic, chaotic Yu gardens and temple.
It's made up of three levels and boasts more
than 100 years of continuous operation.
Queues stretch out the door but do not be
deterred. The line moves quickly. Ask for
the third-floor restaurant, which only serves
dumplings. Breakfast is the best time to
celebrate this delicacy, which we have yet
to truly discover in Australia. Paper-thin
steamed dough is filled with crab and pork
stock, best extracted with a straw; then the
dough is consumed with ginger and rice
vinegar. Best soup dumplings I have ever
enjoyed, especially for breakfast.

Nougatine Bistro
No.3 Zhong Shan Dong Yi Road,
The Bund 200002
☎ +86 21 632 17733
threeonthebund.com/
The organic pork chop wrapped in pancetta
on a bed of mushrooms is considered a 'go-
to' dish by the local Shanghainese.

Ultraviolet
18 the Bund (Meeting Point), 200070
uvbypp.cc
Ultraviolet is possibly the most unique
restaurant dining experience of all time.
A total experience designed to stimulate all
the senses, but you need to book months
in advance via a website. Adding to the
mystery, there is no front door or even
an address. Guests are picked up from
the Bund and driven by luxury coach to
a discreet warehouse in a location I have
sworn on my life not to mention. Paul
Piret, a French local, has been cooking in
various places in Shanghai for more than
ten years and has now nailed his reputation
to the ceiling with the seemingly kooky
but sensorially brilliant idea of combining
video, sound, theatre and smell matched
to a twenty-course menu on the themes of
The Past and The Future. Two menus exist,
UVA and UVB, which alternate weekly.
I want to tell you more but they'd have to
kill me, and in any case explanations are
impossible without spoiling the surprise.
All I can say to you is go.

Xiaoyang Fried Dumpling
Huang He Road, No 97
(near Fengyang Road)
☎ +86 21 53751793
In my view, the best fried dumplings
in Shanghai.

Xindalu at Hyatt on the Bund →
199 Huang Pu Road, 200080
☎ + 86 21 6393 1234
shanghai.bund.hyatt.com/en/hotel/
dining
Really the best Peking duck around but
you must pre-order. The duck is served
differently from the way you might expect.
The skin is so fine that you start with that,
served alone with sugar, and it melts in
your mouth. The breast meat is then
served as a second course, wrapped in
the familiar pancakes.

Ye Olde Station
201 North Caoxi Road, Xújiāhuì
☎ + 86 21 6427 2233
This place is all about traditional Shanghai
food, such as steamed river fish washed
down with a carafe of warm yellow wine.
In the glorious old building that houses the
restaurant you will find two train carriages,
once owned by the last Emperor's mother,
and old meets new with a kitchen vegetable
garden in the centre courtyard.

Singapore

Cuisines from all over Asia come
together and combine with its colonial
heritage in this vivid city.

Food is at the heart and soul of this city; it *is* the culture. Street food is a Singaporean institution. There's a place for high-end restaurants too, but they have to have soul. How many cuisines can one city offer? Here there are Indian, Malay, Southern Chinese, Cantonese, Thai and even colonial influences. The 'everyday cuisine' is Chinese influenced – noodle houses, seafood restaurants and amazing hawker food. Nowhere does chicken and rice better than Singapore.

It's a country smaller in size than Melbourne, and I am amazed at Singapore's resourcefulness, especially given its dependence on others for ingredients. When it comes to food, Singapore knows its strengths. Chefs are not only trained to cook for others; they are now trained to one day have the self-belief, knowledge and fortitude to one day run and operate their own restaurant. The At-Sunrice GlobalChef Academy is a perfect example of this. Miele sponsors scholarships to study at the academy, which also assists the students with careers after graduating. I have been invited to lunch by two former scholarship winners, Malcolm Lee and William Tew Wei Lian, at Guy Savoy, where we enjoy a delicious lunch of local favourites such as sambal petai prawns and butter cereal squid. ●

1 Hand-painted lanterns decorated for the Lantern Festival
2 Durian fruit, famous for its incredibly strong smell, and regarded as a delicacy here.
3 Coffee at Chye Seng Huat Hardware, a converted hardware shop that now sells great coffee.
4–5 Don't be fooled by the plastic chairs and tables – food halls are where you'll find some of the best food in Singapore.

⑦

7–8   We are lucky enough to visit during the
        Lantern Festival, an important part of
        Singapore culture.
9   The city is full of buildings painted in
        these lovely colours, giving the whole place
        a vivid atmosphere.
10   Sri Srinivasa Perumal Temple, Little India.
        There's a strong contingent of Hindus in the
        local population here.

Chilli crab

Serves 4

Every foodie visitor to Singapore is likely to have a great chilli-crab memory. Mine centres around Xing Zhao Ya Ming in Geylang, the city's red-light district. It is without a doubt the only one in the world where men come for the food rather than other more questionable activities.

2 live medium mud crabs, cleaned
¼ teaspoon peanut oil
2 teaspoons vegetable oil
1 egg, lightly beaten
coriander sprigs, to garnish

Chilli paste
2 brown onions, roughly chopped
4 small red chillies, chopped
½ cup (125 ml) grapeseed oil
40 g shrimp paste
200 ml pureed tomato
200 ml Heinz tomato ketchup
¼ cup (60 ml) light soy sauce
50 g white sugar
3 tablespoons well washed and chopped
    coriander stems
1 tablespoon tomato paste (puree)
2 teaspoons white vinegar
lime juice and sea salt, to taste

To make the chilli paste, place the onion, chilli, grapeseed oil, shrimp paste, pureed tomato, ketchup, soy sauce, sugar, coriander stems, tomato paste and vinegar in a blender or a powerful food processor and blend together. Season to taste with lime juice and salt. Spoon into an airtight container until needed.

If you like, you can make the paste a few days in advance and store it in the fridge.

About 30 minutes before you are ready to cook, put the live crabs in the freezer to put them to sleep.

Preheat the steamer to 90°C.

Cut the crabs in half using a sharp knife, then crack the large part of the claws with the back of the knife. Break off all the large claws and cut them in half. Cut the bodies into quarters. Place all the crab pieces in the steamer tray and steam for 9 minutes.

Heat a wok over a wok induction set on 9 or a gas burner over medium–high heat. When the wok is smoking, add the oils, then quickly add all the pieces of crab and toss the wok several times. (If you are using an induction, simply keep the wok on the induction and stir with a spatula.) Add about half the paste (more if the crabs are large) and the beaten egg and stir-fry for 1 minute. Transfer to a serving plate or bowl, garnish with a few sprigs of coriander and serve immediately.

Oyster omelette

Serves 4

Cooked oysters release a wonderful flavour –
I really wish people would eat more of them at
home. This omelette is another street food classic,
found in all hawker markets (my favourite being
from the market below the Singapore Flyer).
I actually had Corey make this dish the first time
to test the recipe. It tasted sensational but looked
way too perfect! This is comfort food and should
be served nice and relaxed.

¼ cup (60 ml) vegetable oil
1 clove garlic, finely chopped
¼ cup (35 g) potato flour mixed with
    ½ cup (125 ml) water
8 eggs, lightly beaten
8 local oysters, freshly shucked
2 pinches of sea salt
pinch of freshly ground white pepper
1 teaspoon Chinese cooking wine
1 spring onion, thinly sliced
coriander leaves, to garnish (optional)
light soy sauce, to serve

Heat a wok over a wok induction set on 8 or a gas
burner over medium–high heat. When the wok is
smoking, add the vegetable oil and garlic, then add
the potato flour paste and cook for 30 seconds.

Pour the beaten egg into the wok and leave for
1 minute to set, then vigorously stir, chopping up
the egg. Add the oysters, salt, pepper and cooking
wine. Taste and season if needed.

Divide among plates and garnish with spring
onion and coriander (if using). Serve immediately
with light soy sauce on the side.

Bur bur cha cha

Serves 4

David Thompson first made bur bur cha cha for me at Sailors Thai in Sydney and I fell in love with it. But this is a Peranakan recipe. What is Peranakan? A sublime marriage of Malaysian and Chinese cultures, and therefore cuisines. This simple soup consists of coconut, tapioca, yam, sweet potato and dehydrated sago seeds. I was inspired to document this recipe by chef William. He arrived at the Gallery bright and early with fresh coconuts, which he then hand-grated before painstakingly crushing the flesh in a mortar and pestle, and squeezing it through a piece of cheese cloth to extract the milk. Now that's what I call commitment! Tapioca takes longer to steam than yam and sweet potato so give it a little more time. If yam and sweet potato are not your cup of tea, just add any fruit you desire. The sago seeds need to soak overnight so start this recipe the day before you want to serve it.

50 g dehydrated sago seeds
200 g caster sugar
2 cups (500 ml) water
1 bunch pandan leaves, tied into a bunch
100 g young yam, peeled and roughly chopped
100 g sweet potato, peeled and
    roughly chopped
100 g fresh tapioca, peeled and
    roughly chopped
400 ml coconut milk, plus extra if needed
2½–3 tablespoons cooked red beans

Soak the sago seeds in water overnight. Drain.

Preheat the steamer to 100% steam.

Make a sugar syrup by combining the sugar and water in a medium saucepan. Bring to the boil, add the bunch of pandan, and then remove from the heat and leave to infuse for 30 minutes.

Meanwhile, steam the root vegetables until tender, then leave to cool to room temperature.

Remove the pandan from the sugar syrup and discard. Add the root vegetables and sago seeds and stir in the coconut milk. Adjust the consistency by adding more coconut milk if you prefer a thicker soup – personally I like mine to be quite thin.

Sprinkle the red beans into 4 bowls and spoon the soup over the top. I like to serve it at room temperature, but you could also have it hot or cold.

Visitor tips

The best
fish head curry

The iconic Singaporean dishes are chicken and rice, and chilli crab, and then there is the lesser known but equally iconic fish head curry. All three, alone, put Singapore on the map for being a great food destination, but where do you go for the best? This question will always prompt arguments, but for me, you can't go wrong at places like The Banana Leaf Apolo, Muthu's Curry on Racecourse Road and Samy's Curry Restaurant. All three are sensational. In Singapore the curry is done either Indian-style or Chinese-style; these restaurants serve the Indian style where the fish head sits in a rich curry sauce with vegetables and I simply cannot go past it.

Desserts

2am:dessertbar
21A Lorong Liput, 277733
☎ +65 6291 9727
2amdessertbar.com
Holland Village plays host to Janice Wong's dessert bar, where she and her team create different themed à la carte menus featuring desserts. There are some savoury items such as small burgers (sliders) where all the ingredients, including the cheese, are made by Janice's team. Open to 2 a.m. every day except Sunday, when it is closed. Edible art is a hobby of Janice's; she has made everything from a marshmallow ceiling to marshmallow and chocolate handbags.

Hotels

The Capella
1 The Knolls, Sentosa Island, 098297
☎ +65 6377 8888
capellahotels.com/singapore
Set on Sentosa Island, fifteen minutes from the city centre by taxi (around $10). When the concrete jungle of the city gets too much, you can retreat to your very own, very large room and a balcony overlooking the harbour and its dozens of container ships waiting to unload. The main hotel lobby and library is positioned in an old colonial building surrounded by several acres of gardens. A rooftop bar and pool completes this hotel, putting it among my favourites; in fact if I'm travelling with the family it is the only hotel in Singapore I stay at. Be sure to take advantage of the proximity to Joel Robuchon's restaurant in the casino, walking distance from the hotel. Don't be deterred by the tackiness of the casino; Robuchon's is a seriously great fine-dining French restaurant for that serious night out, or a nibble in the bar. The kids will also love the beach and the many activities associated.

Fullerton Bay Hotel
80 Collyer Quay, 049326
☎ +65 6333 8388
fullertonbayhotel.com
I had confused this hotel with the Fullerton Hotel, which is no slouch in its own right, but the Fullerton Bay is a whole other proposition. Once you check in here you know that you are experiencing privilege at its finest. Rooms closest to the water have the greatest privacy from walkers, joggers and the odd gaggle of tourists. Rooms are large and opulent.

The Majestic →
31–37 Bukit Pasoh Road, 089845
☎ +65 6511 4700
newmajestichotel.com
One of the first boutique hotels to start up here. Hotelier Loh Lik Peng has a good eye for detail. Well priced and well positioned on a quiet back street in Chinatown. The suites are exceptional, utilising the ultra-high ceilings to create mezzanine levels. The gym is compact but one of the best I have trained in for its size. Staff for the most part are very enthusiastic but don't expect five-star concierge service; that is not why you are here. There is no cafeteria-style breakfast dining either. Just pure moments of contentment, sitting out on the front lawn of the hotel at dusk, tossing up between a whisky sour or a martini.

Park Royal on Pickering
3 Upper Pickering St, 058289
☎ +65 6809 8888
parkroyalhotels.com/Pickering
Exceptional value with great design. Rooms are generally small, but that said, are really well designed with super comfy beds. Request a corner room on the marina side, looking out over Clarke Quay. Also ask for access to the club lounge floor.

The Ritz Carlton
7 Raffles Ave
☎ +65 6337 8888
ritzcarlton.com
Located within metres of the marina. Be sure to push for an upgrade to a corner suite. The views from floors ten and above are extraordinary. The hexagonal windows look out over the gardens by the bay. Staff are top notch and the Japanese restaurant is also not to be scoffed at. Avoid breakfast in the restaurant – it is overcrowded and the only downside here, reminding me of an old-style executive staff cafeteria.

Markets/street food

Ah Heng Curry Chicken 'Bee Hoon Mee' at the Maxwell Centre
1 Kadayanallur St
yoursingapore.com/content/traveller/
en/browse/dining/restaurants/
maxwell-road-hawker-centre.html
Exciting, colourful, eclectic, busy, delicious and good value. The prices can only be described as cheap! A large bowl of spiced chicken broth, slivers of fish cake, two types of noodle, accurately poached chicken breast and crispy tofu all served in a white plastic bowl amongst the bustle of a food market bonanza, for only $6. There are two acceptable thirst quenchers in this part of the world: crushed sugar cane juice or ice-cold Tiger beer, and you will find a bottomless supply of both here.

All Airport Road Hawker Centre
Block 51, Old Airport Rd, Geylang
This place embodies perfectly everything that's good about this city. Open until the early hours of the morning on weekends, with big crowds congregating particularly around the oyster omelette stand and Xin Mei Xiang Lor Mee, a noodle stand. You can't go wrong with any of the thirty-plus stalls here, though. All you need to do is turn up and be hungry.

Golden Mile Beach Road Thai Food
5001 Beach Rd, 199588
Also known as Little Thailand, this is reputed to be the best Thai in Singapore. I have a soft spot for the area; there's incense in the air and the buzz of different languages being belted out. A must-visit.

Lau Sat Pau Hawker Centre
18 Raffles Quay (Downtown Core)
best-singapore-guide.com/
Lau-Pa-Sat.html
My all-round favourite hawker centre, best known for its Indian food and everything pig – from stir-fried with black pepper to pigs' intestine soup. This very large market is under cover and is always full of people, and there's live music at night. Try to avoid the lunchtime rush.

Pasarbella Food Market
200 Turf Club Rd, 287994
☎ +65 6887 0077
pasarbella.com
For something very different, and to get out of the city centre if you're spending more than a couple of days here, try Pasarbella. Set on a disused race course called Turf City, it's a local attempt at the farmers' market concept but better. It reminds me of New York's Chelsea markets.

Tekka Market, Little India
665 Buffalo Rd, 210665
yoursingapore.com/content/traveller/
en/browse/shopping/shop-by-category/
ethnic-finds/tekka-centre.html
Colour, atmosphere and the best-quality produce in Singapore, available direct to the public. Look out for a local seller right at the end of the street called Chai, selling what many chefs say is the best and widest array of vegetables in the city. I suggest chefs or avid foodies go before 7 a.m. as that is when it is at its busiest but the stalls are still full. It stays open up until about 3 p.m.

Restaurants

Tetsuya's Waku Gin
Atrium 2, Level 2, Marina Bay Sands,
10 Bayfront Avenue, 018956
☎ +65 6688 8507
marinabaysands.com
All I can remember is the peach. I have no idea where in Japan Tetsuya found these peaches; all I remember him telling me was that I was lucky to be enjoying it. He only gets fifty a year. Served barley-poached, with raspberry sauce and the most delicate vanilla ice cream (better described as super-cold whipped cream), it was the best dessert I've ever eaten. The place is in a very large, tacky casino but don't let that put you off; once inside you feel as if you are in Tetsuya's house. This is his dream space and you can taste it in the food. Every dish has purpose, inspired by the two countries he loves, Japan and Australia.

Xing Zhao Ya Ming
In Geylang (Red Light District)
Hands down the best Asian seafood you will find in Singapore. Sure, it is down a small lane in a car park in the middle of the red light district but hey, when you eat the most perfectly fried noodles with crispy cereal-coated baby prawns, smoky wok-fried steamed lobster and crispy shallots smothering steamed razor clams, washed down with a cold beer in the open air on plastic tables in a great atmosphere with great company, who's complaining?

Toronto

With a strong French influence,
this city also features cuisines
as diverse as Ethiopian and Filipino.

This town is not made for tourists, it is made for its people. We arrive late in Toronto and are picked up by Marc, who takes me on a quick tour before I check in to my hotel. Toronto is the home of the first ever Four Seasons, so I found it appropriate to rest my head in this fine establishment. The original hotel is a block away, now converted into apartments; the one I'm staying in was opened only two years ago. The feel is modern and not overcrowded although the bar can be loud. It makes for a nice vibe, packed with local twenty-something trendsetters. Cafe Boulud, by renowned New York chef, Daniel Boulud, is one of the most celebrated restaurants in town, and the hotel bar also has his name on the door. My late-night snack in the room is very good: Nova Scotia lobster salad, reasonably cheap at C$26 if you overlook the obligatory 20 per cent tip plus a delivery charge to the room! Locally brewed beers are big in Ontario and feature on tap in the bar. My favourites are the lager styles, such as Cheshire Valley.

It feels as if my head has barely graced the pillow before it is morning. On a positive note, there is nothing better than a 5 a.m. jog to really see this city. The choppy footpaths take me inland towards Queens Street, the place for off-the-beaten-track clothing stores, and independent outlets of every item you need if you are twenty and have no room left on your neck and arms for tattoos. I love the vibe, even at 6 a.m. with only a couple of cafes and the famous blues venue The Rex open. I stop for a quick coffee at a place called the Dark Horse Espresso. It's really good. The guys on the machine have an intense passion for their product. I realise later, after a fruitless search for other independent cafes, that there are none so Dark Horse wins out for the best coffee in the area.

I decide to try a different hotel, as I want something closer to Queen Street and a little more action. I check in to the new Shangri-la Hotel, located smack-bang in the middle of downtown on University Avenue. By sheer luck I score an upgrade to the sixteenth floor. My one-bedroom suite is as modern and decadent as they come. ➜

1   The striking Gooderham Building, an early example of a 'flatiron' building, and one of Toronto's most famous landmarks.

2–3   The Queen Mother Cafe – how can you resist a name like that?

4   Old City Hall. It's been threatened with demolition serveral times but the citizens of Toronto's affection for it is so great, they have succeeded in preserving it.

Next to the hotel is the four-level Korean-inspired restaurant chain Momofuku, by David Chang. I drop in to the noodle bar on the ground floor. Chang is famous for his steamed pork buns, a personal weak spot of mine. The menu changes daily; I start with the buns and simply put they are 'bloody beautiful'. Two types of ramen noodles follow: the classic smoked chicken, topped with a perfectly cooked egg and pickled shiitake mushrooms, and flavoured with miso broth. The other, which I ordered because I was missing Shanghai, was described on the menu as 'very very hot noodles' and it wasn't wrong!

I decide to make a dinner booking the next night (after we have cooked for a mere forty people, that is!) at his third-floor restaurant Shoto. At C$150 for ten courses, it seems great value for what most locals say is the best restaurant in Toronto. The food is very good and it's well worth visiting.

Dinner that night is at Bar Isabel on College Street. Many of the people I speak to vote it their favourite restaurant. I am intrigued by the Spanish tapas concept, which is huge in Melbourne and Sydney, mainly due to the Movida brand. Bar Isabel is a little out of the city centre but don't let that deter you. The food and ambience here is great. So is the area; it's in the heart of little Portugal, which is crammed with superb, intimate bars and restaurants.

The next morning the team and I are joined by Dr Reinhard Zinkann at St Lawrence Market, rated the number one market in the world by *National Geographic* in 2012. We are all intrigued by this accolade. We are relieved to find it is an indoor farmers' market as it is freezing outside. The main attraction here is the ready-to-eat food, especially the Pea Meal Bacon sandwich from the Carousel Bakery. It should be mandatory when visiting St Lawrence to try one. They are simple and good. It's a Toronto specialty; originally pork loin was cured with brown sugar and then rolled in crushed yellow peas. In this version the pea meal has been replaced by corn maize. ➜

5–6   At Momofuku Toronto.
7–8   Dinner at Bar Isabel in the heart of
        Little Portugal.
9   Toronto at dusk, viewed from my hotel room.

Six layers of bacon are stacked on top and the whole thing is crammed into a soft round roll with maple mustard. Worth getting here in the early morning when an egg and some cheese is added. It is Toronto's version of a bacon butty.

The small market is a real gem in the heart of the city. The land left vacant by the former tobacco industry has been turned by local farmers into food crops, flooding the market with incredible produce and changing the culture of local chefs. Most chefs pop down to pick up small quantities of items they cannot get delivered so it is both strange and exciting to see so many chefs in their jackets wandering around. Canadian cheese is also a great surprise; try it if you get a chance. On the way out, we buy a pound of local wild musk ox to play around with for a recipe idea I have. Not far up from the market, a small place called Richmond Station does a good pea meal bun with rosemary fries.

Close by, we head up to Canoe, a bar and restaurant on the fifty-fourth floor of the TD Bank Tower, well known to Ontarians. Its greatest asset is the incredible view. Great Canadian wine list. There's an incredible view of the lake – really more of an inland sea.

Toronto stays true to the cultures it represents. This is a city where most citizens speak French as a second language, yet you could not buy a cliched croissant or French onion soup to save yourself. Instead you can feast on *tourtiere*, a version of the classic meat pie, but with high-quality ground beef with spices. *Poutine* is a classic French–Canadian dish of hot chips, beef gravy and cheese curds. Trust me, it tastes better than it sounds!

Here you can also eat some of the best Ethiopian food in the world. Every bite I put in my mouth seems to honour its place of origin. Toronto is made up of very distinctive pockets of ethnic groups, the largest being the Hong Kong Chinese and then the Eastern Indians. Cultural diversity is really the key to this city's food. I must say I have never been to a Filipino restaurant before but when in Toronto there are actually a few to choose from. ●

10–11 Shopping at St Lawrence Market, where many local chefs get their supplies.
12–13 The Carousel Bakery and a friendly cheese-maker at the St Lawrence Markets. I was really impressed by the quality of the cheese.
14 The back of the Gooderham Building, decorated with a stunning trompe l'oeil painting to make it look as if it has more windows.

Musk ox tartare with yukon gold potatoes and pickles

Serves 4

Musk oxen were nearly extinct a few decades ago but now there are over 100 000 roaming free in northern Canada. I was intrigued enough by this incredible-looking animal to test out the flavour that is lauded by so many. Needless to say, I was not disappointed. You may need to pre-order the bison tenderloin from your butcher, so check with them first.

2 tablespoons goose fat
sea salt
4 medium roasting potatoes
    (preferably yukon gold, otherwise sebago),
    peeled and cut into 3 mm thick slices
200 g bison tenderloin, finely diced
1 golden shallot, finely diced
1 tablespoon dijon mustard
1 tablespoon worcestershire sauce
¼ cup (60 ml) tomato passata
1 teaspoon tabasco sauce
2–3 tablespoons roughly chopped
    flat-leaf parsley
1 teaspoon freshly ground black pepper,
    plus extra if needed
4 quail eggs
cornichons, to serve

Heat a heavy frying pan over an induction set on 6 or a gas burner over medium heat, and add the goose fat and a good pinch of salt. Add the potato slices and cook until golden and crispy on both sides. Remove from the pan and keep warm.

Combine the bison meat, shallot, mustard, worcestershire, passata, tabasco, parsley and pepper in a bowl. Taste and adjust the seasoning if needed.

Divide the tartare among 4 boards or bowls, then make a small indent in the middle with the back of a spoon. Crack a quail egg into each indent and season with salt and pepper. Serve with the warm crispy potatoes and cornichons to the side – encourage your guests to use the potatoes to scoop up the tartare.

Grilled lobster with hollandaise and smoked sausage

Serves 2

We all love a lobster recipe, don't we? This one is perfect for that romantic dinner for 2 at home. Mind you, because most of the preparation can be done in advance, it can also cater for larger numbers – simply finish it off under a very hot grill before serving. Some of the best lobster on the planet comes from Nova Scotia but if, like me, you live in on the other side of the world and can't always source great lobster, bay bugs or crayfish make a good substitute.

1 × 800 g local live lobster or crayfish
iced water
1 tablespoon grapeseed oil
2 tablespoons finely diced seeded red
    capsicum (pepper)
100 g hot smoked sausage, roughly chopped
sea salt and freshly ground black pepper
lemon cheeks, to serve

Hollandaise sauce
3 egg yolks
1 tablespoon champagne vinegar
200 g cultured butter, melted
1 tablespoon chopped tarragon
juice of ¼ lemon, or to taste
sea salt

Place the lobster in the freezer for 30 minutes so it goes to sleep.

Preheat the steamer to 100°C. Steam the lobster for 9 minutes, then remove and immerse it in iced water for 10 minutes to stop the cooking process.

Remove the lobster from the water and drain well. Place the lobster on a chopping board with the underside of the body facing upwards and split the body and tail in half lengthways. Carefully remove the meat from each tail half. Slice each tail half into 4 pieces, then place back in the opposite tail shell so the red part of the flesh is facing upwards. Transfer the lobster to a baking tray, facing upwards.

To make the hollandaise sauce, bring a saucepan of water to the boil then reduce to a simmer. Place the egg yolks and vinegar in a metal bowl over the saucepan and whisk until light and fluffy. Remove the bowl from the saucepan and slowly add the melted butter, whisking constantly to reach a thick consistency. Add the tarragon and lemon juice to taste, then season to taste with salt.

Preheat the oven on fan grill to 240°C.

Heat the grapeseed oil in a frying pan over an induction set on 6 or a gas burner over medium heat. Add the capsicum and cook for 2–3 minutes, then add the sausage and lobster meat and saute for 1 minute. Transfer to a bowl and season lightly with salt and pepper.

Fill the head part of the shells with the sausage and capsicum mixture. Spoon the hollandaise sauce over the entire half from head to tail. Grill the lobster halves for 2–3 minutes or until golden. Serve immediately with lemon cheeks.

Quick maple syrup mousse with caramelised nuts and blistered blueberries

Serves 4

Now here's something I bet you didn't know: Canada produces and exports more blueberries than anywhere else in the world. I found them bigger, sweeter and juicier than any I had ever tasted before. And how can I celebrate Canadian produce without including maple syrup? This mousse is very easy to make but it does require a cream whip gun. They are available in most good homeware and kitchenware stores.

3 × 3 g gold gelatine leaves
700 ml cream
8 egg yolks
200 ml maple syrup
125 g caster sugar
150 g pecans
150 g skinned hazelnuts
60 g raw sugar
500 g blueberries
1 tablespoon water

Soak the gelatine in iced water for 15 minutes.

Pour the cream into a medium heavy-based saucepan and place over medium heat. As soon as it comes to the boil, remove the pan from the heat.

In a stainless steel bowl, lightly whisk the egg yolks to ribbon stage, then carefully whisk in the hot cream. Squeeze out any excess water from the gelatine leaves and whisk into the cream mixture until dissolved, then set aside to cool for 10 minutes. Gently fold in the maple syrup. Using a funnel, pour the mixture into a cream whip gun, charge with 2 gas bulbs and shake well.

Preheat the oven on the conventional setting 140°C. Scatter the pecans and hazelnuts on a baking tray and gently roast for 10–12 minutes or until light golden in colour.

Heat a medium heavy-based saucepan over an induction set on 6 (gas is not recommended) and add the caster sugar to the pan. When it starts to melt and caramelise, reduce the induction level to 4 and cook until the caramel is a medium golden colour. Add the nuts, then remove from the heat and stir until the caramel and nuts are fully incorporated. Pour the mixture onto a clean work surface or a tray lined with baking paper and leave to cool and set. When the caramel is firm, break it into small to medium chunks and set aside.

The final step is to make the blistered blueberries. Using the same saucepan, add the raw sugar and let it melt over medium heat. Stir in the blueberries then, when they start to puff and split open, add the water to deglaze the pan. Remove from the heat and keep warm in the pan.

Layer the mousse, blueberries and caramelised nuts twice into a large serving bowl or individual bowls, finishing with the nuts. Serve at room temperature or keep in the fridge for later use.

Visitor tips

Casual eateries

Banh Mi Boys
392 Queen Street West
☎ +1 416 363 0588
banhmiboys.com
Best grilled pork bahn mi in town.

Mata Hari Grill
39 Baldwin Street, M5T 1L1
☎ +1 416 596 2832
mataharigrill.com
Locals describe this place as 'spectacular
Malaysian'.

Rodney's Oyster House
469 King Street West
☎ +1 416 363-8105
rodneysoysterhouse.com
Casual dining and great fresh seafood.
We've never had a bad meal there.

Smoke's Poutinerie
218 Adelaide Street, West Toronto
☎ +1 416 599 2873
smokespoutinerie.com
This place does the poutine with a twist,
using different meats and cheeses. The
pulled pork poutine is a winner!

Hotels

The Baldwin Inn
9 Baldwin St, M5T 1L1
☎ +1 416 591 5359
baldwininn.com
The Baldwin is as small as it is charming –
there are only six rooms – but it's the
location that makes it stand out. An oasis
in the centre of downtown Toronto,
Baldwin Village has more good restaurants
than you could choose from in a week
of dining out, all of them within 100 metres
of the front door.

The Roof Lounge, Park Hyatt
4 Avenue Rd, M5R 2E8
☎ +1 416 925 1234
parktoronto.hyatt.com/en/hotel/dining/
TheRoofLounge.html
Centrally located and well priced for a
very high-end hotel. The place to be for
star-spotting during the ten nights of
the Toronto International Film Festival
in September. Big celebrities like Matt
Damon and George Clooney don't stay
here, but who needs Hollywood when
you have a rooftop bar, great weather and
smart, inventive cocktails? Be warned, it's
a little dated and you need to get there
early for the good seats. But it is the best
view in town.

The tourist checklist

While you are here in Toronto it's
compulsory to check out two of the
most fascinating buildings in the world.
The Ontario College of Art and Design
(OCAD) is breathtaking, balanced on
stilts six stories up in the air, and Frank
Gehry's Art Gallery of Ontario is another
extraordinarily brave building! Check out
the spiral stairs inside.

Niagara Falls
6039 Fallsview Blvd, Niagara Falls,
L2G 3V9
☎ +1 866 663 9435
niagarafallstourstoronto.com
A comfortable one-hour drive from the
city centre is the most iconic waterfall
in the world. A must for any tourist. The
quaint, picturesque village of Niagara-on-
the-Lake is also home to some great dining
destinations, Treadwell being the best.
Steven Treadwell, chef and owner, makes
a meal here worth the journey in itself.

Out of town

Eigensinn Farm
2 Farm Gate Rd., 449357 10th
Concession, Singhampton, ON N0C 1M0
☎ +1 519 922 3128
eigensinnfarm.blogspot.com
Eigensinn Farm is the home of the culinary
icon Michael Stadtländer. *Stagiaires*, chefs
who work for free to gain experience, flock
to his restaurant to gather knowledge on
true farm-to-plate cooking. They grow and
raise their own vegetables and livestock
and cook multi-course menus. Stadtländer
is a pioneer in the world of restaurants.
He has turned his ranch house into
a dining venue for discerning foodies while
introducing the idea of agrotourism to
Canada. Approximately ninety minutes'
drive north from the centre of Toronto.
The restaurant is not licensed so remember
to BYO.

Vienna

A city of art, old and new, with a lively
bar scene and plenty of cakes to balance
out the city's love of cycling.

Jogging or walking is the perfect way to see any city, but Vienna is tough as there is no grid system to the streets, which is what makes it so special at the same time! Combine hesitation, natural rubbernecking, and one-sixth of the population on bikes riding very fast at any one time and you have the potential to get very lost, very quickly. Head for the canal, approximately one kilometre from St Stephen's cathedral. Once you hit the water, you see the city's younger side, with a flourishing community of pop-up diners, grills and bars. I especially like Holy Moly, created by chef Christian Petz who gave up the world of fine dining to open a groovy bar/diner serving local food to a young, hip audience craving change aboard, of all things, a disused ferry. Tel Aviv is also worth a visit and there are also terrific bistro/event spaces dotted along the riverbank. Tel Aviv has a funky outdoor beer garden opposite an outdoor gym. It's all about balance. Street art also features heavily on both sides of the canal. The place hums with brooding excitement, anticipation, potential. It is all new to me; my eyes are being opened to the thrilling dichotomy of this city where two worlds collide: the old happily coexisting alongside the new.

Jogging further along the canal I reach the spot where it opens on to the Danube, framed by stacked rock walls leading to lush grassy banks perfect for stretching out upon and cloud-watching. Passing numerous bike repair shops with small bars attached, I'm struck again by the seeming contradiction of this place, where exercise seems to be automatically cancelled out by the offer of indulgence on site, but which really, as I'm coming to understand, promotes a balanced lifestyle. What better way to cap off a session pumping iron than relaxing over a fine drop with friends, listening to some tunes in the beer garden. And I would be more inspired to wear out the treads putting some miles behind me on the bike if I knew the local pit stop would lure me in for a cold pilsner while replacing my wheels. It all makes perfect sense to me! ➔

1   The view from the hotel window. Whichever angle you look at this city from, you'll see something beautiful.

2–4   There's street art everywhere and even a rusty old sign forbidding entry looks artistic.

5   Holy Moly, the bar, nightclub and swimming pool created from a disused ferry.

6   The Holy Trinity Plague Column. This extravagant gilded sculpture adorned with angels and other celestial beings was built in the hope of warding off plague.

Strudel

Gerstner is without a doubt one of Vienna's, if not the world's, most famous coffee houses, best known for its strudel and Viennese cakes. Founded by Anton Gerstner in 1847, the shop is also well known for catering for the New Year opera ball.

Viennese cafes are places you go to linger, not pop in for a quick coffee, and the proprietors get more than a little grumpy if you don't follow this protocol.

After taking a few bites I was hooked, ready to stand up and yodel for my dessert like the best of 'em! The pastry is the key, stretched to paper thinness.

Strudel is not limited to sliced apple but whatever is in season; when we visit they are filling them with plum, and apricot production is also about to start. It is probably the most difficult cake to bake at home but many Austrians still attempt them on weekends.

There are currently 270 varieties of apple grown in Austria. The most popular come from the area called Styria. The raisins are soaked in Austrian rum for twenty-four hours. The rest is all about technique. Toasted breadcrumbs are combined with brown sugar to absorb the cooking juices from the drunken apples. →

7–8 With some of the Gerstner pastry chefs, seasoning apples for strudel.

9–10 At Cafe Sperl, one of Vienna's grand old cafes. These are places to read the newspaper and engage in intense philosophical discussions over a lengthy coffee.

11   Medusa heads guard the entrance to the
      Secession Palace, now a museum of art. The
      three heads represent three art forms: painting,
      sculpture and architecture.
12   A glimpse of the magnificent Hofburg Palace
      from the street.
13   A statue built in honour of King Franz Josef
      I, his wife and child, outside the Albertine
      Museum Palace.
14   Mosaic planters, supported by little turtles,
      outside the Secession Palace art museum.
15–16 They are serious about their cakes here in
      Vienna, and Cafe Sperl has some of the best.

Living room off the street

The Grand Cafe Weimar, built in 1880, is owned by legendary local identity Maximilian Platzer. It is a place for making new relationships, rebuilding old ones and rekindling existing ones, and where business deals are conducted on wooden benches padded with ornate velvet, usually in inconspicuous corners.

Door frames are made of spectacular carved wood. There are glistening chandeliers and a gold clock that can be seen from everywhere in the dining room. The Austro–Hungarian empire brought this type of cafe culture to the people of Vienna and it will never leave. Reading the newspaper over a coffee with a splash of local rum or schnapps thrown in and topped with a little whipped cream in decor that has not changed since the mid-1900s feels downright magical. Semolina dumpling, a Viennese obsession, is a specialty in this coffee house.

Cafe life is so important here, as Max intones: 'My customers may sit on luxury velvet with a glass of water all day if they want. This is people's living rooms.' ●

17   A stunning painted archway in the Museum Quarter.
18   Bakery Joseph – Brot Vom Pheinsten, where what I believe to be the finest sourdough bread in Europe is produced.
19–21 At Cafe Weimar, another Vienna institution. It may look quite formal but people are welcome to spend as long as they like here; cafe culture is integral to the city's way of life.

Wiener schnitzel

Serves 4

This is as traditional as it gets in Viennese cuisine. Crumbing the meat is what makes or breaks this dish, and there is an actual science behind its perfection. If the meat is completely coated in crumbs, it is unable to escape from its jacket during frying, resulting in a souffle-type effect. It's a real education – you simply don't get this level of refinement for the humble schnitzel in Australia.

4 × 200 g pieces trimmed veal silverside
sea salt and freshly ground black pepper
1 cup (150 g) plain flour
4 eggs
2½ cups (250 g) dried breadcrumbs
vegetable oil or clarified butter,
    for pan-frying
lemon halves or wedges, to serve

Butterfly each piece of veal with a sharp knife, then place between 2 sheets of plastic film and pound gently to an even thickness. Season well on both sides.

Tip the flour onto a plate, and whisk the eggs with a fork in a shallow bowl. Tip the breadcrumbs onto another plate. Coat both sides of the schnitzel pieces in flour, then egg, then gently toss in the breadcrumbs, pressing down slightly to make sure they are well coated with no gaps. Crumb them twice for a really crisp finish.

Pour the vegetable oil or clarified butter into a large frying pan to a depth of 5 cm and heat over high heat. Add the schnitzels (in batches if necessary) and cook for 1½ minutes each side or until well browned and cooked through. Drain on paper towel to remove any excess oil, then serve immediately with lemon to squeeze over.

Clear beef soup with semolina dumplings

Serves 4

This is a very typical Austrian soup – all the vegetables you'll need are usually sold in one packet at the markets. It's really easy to make and has a great meaty flavour. The marrow bones need to soak overnight so start this recipe the day before you need it.

**4 pieces beef marrow bone
    (with the marrow still inside)**
**400 g beef tri-tip (or rump),
    cut into 4 pieces**
**2 medium yellow carrots, trimmed
    and sliced into rounds**
**2 medium orange carrots, trimmed and
    sliced into rounds**
1 celeriac, trimmed and sliced into rounds
**2 brown onions, cut in half, peeled and
    thinly sliced**
2 cloves garlic, peeled
½ bunch flat-leaf parsley roots
**5 dried pimento berries (also known as
    Jamaica pepper)**
4 bay leaves
sea salt
3 litres water, plus extra to refill
2 tablespoons finely chopped chives

Semolina dumplings
1¼ cups (200 g) semolina
2 eggs, lightly beaten
75 g butter
freshly grated nutmeg
sea salt and freshly ground black pepper

Soak the marrow bones in cold water overnight to get rid of any blood left in the bone.

Place all the ingredients (except the chives) in a deep stainless steel container. Preheat the steamer to 100% steam and cook for 2 hours. Refill the container with water and steam for a further 1 hour. (Using the steamer will result in a perfectly clear soup, but you could also put all the ingredients in a large saucepan and simmer for 3 hours.)

To make the semolina dumplings, place all the ingredients in a bowl and mix well. Cover and rest for at least 1 hour.

The next step is to make quenelles. To do this, hold a dessertspoon in each hand, take a spoonful of the dumpling mixture then, using the other spoon, scoop the mixture off the first spoon, turning it slightly as you do so to achieve a smooth almond shape. Repeat the process until it is even on all sides. You should have enough mixture to make 8 dumplings. Store them in the fridge until the soup is ready.

Strain the soup through a fine-mesh sieve. Keep the vegetables – you can serve them as a garnish, although the soup is traditionally served just with the beef and dumplings.

Transfer the strained soup to a clean saucepan. Drop the dumplings into the soup and simmer gently for 10 minutes or until they are cooked through.

Divide the soup and dumplings among 4 bowls and finish with a sprinkling of chives. Serve the beef and bone marrow separately or in the soup.

Apple strudel

Serves 4

Many of us have aspired to make a strudel dough at some stage. Although it may seem daunting, the dough itself is based on quite a simple technique of stretching the gluten in the flour to its limits. There is nothing wrong with sneaking in a YouTube session on the subject before making your first attempt – actually seeing the technique is really helpful.

50 g butter, melted
icing sugar, for dusting
cream, to serve

Spiced apples
½ cup (75 g) raisins
100 ml rum
1 lemon
750 g firm, sour apples (such as idared or golden delicious)
50 g vanilla sugar
50 g caster sugar
2 teaspoons ground cinnamon

Strudel dough
125 g plain flour
pinch of sea salt
1½ tablespoons vegetable oil
¼ cup (60 ml) water

Sugared breadcrumbs
80 g butter
160 g dried breadcrumbs
1 tablespoon raw sugar

To start preparing the spiced apples, soak the raisins in the rum overnight.

To make the strudel dough, place all the ingredients in an electric mixer fitted with the hook attachment. Mix slowly for about 10 minutes or until a firm but smooth dough forms. Transfer to a lightly floured bowl and cover with plastic film, then place the dough in the fridge to rest for at least 1 hour, or preferably overnight.

If you don't have an electric mixer, put the flour and salt in a large bowl, make a well in the centre and pour in the oil and 2½ tablespoons water. Gather the dough together and knead by hand, gradually adding the remaining water. If the dough is a little wet, add a touch of flour. You want to reach a consistency where the dough comes away from the bowl without sticking. Cover and rest in the fridge, as above.

To prepare the sugared breadcrumbs, melt the butter in a frying pan over medium heat, add the breadcrumbs and cook until nicely golden. Stir in the sugar and set aside.

Back to the spiced apples. Squeeze the lemon juice into a bowl of water. Peel and core the apples, then cut each one into 6 pieces. Slice each piece into 2–3 mm thick slices and place in the lemon water as you go to stop them going brown. When you're finished, drain the apples and place in a large bowl with the vanilla sugar, caster sugar and cinnamon. Drain the excess rum from the raisins, then stir the raisins through the apple mixture.

Preheat the oven on the conventional setting to 200°C and lightly grease a baking tray. If your dough has been in the refrigerator overnight, take it out 30 minutes before you need to use it.

To assemble the strudel, place the dough on a lightly floured clean piece of linen (it should be about 100 cm × 60 cm) and press out to flatten a little. Continue working around the dough in a circular motion, gently stretching the edges with your fingers. Repeat this process, without making any holes, until you have a very thin sheet of dough.

Gently lay the pastry on the floured linen and stretch it over the edges of the table. Trim the pastry into a regular rectangle about 60 cm × 30 cm, taking off about 2 cm from the edges as this will become very tough. Liberally brush melted butter over the entire sheet of dough.

Sprinkle two-thirds of the breadcrumbs over one end of the dough to cover about one quarter of the length, leaving a 3 cm border at each side. Drain the spiced apple mixture and spoon it evenly over the breadcrumbs. Sprinkle the remaining breadcrumbs on top.

Using the linen as leverage, quickly roll and flip the dough with the apples, so that you begin to form a large log. Tuck in any bits of apple that may have spilled out. Continue rolling to the end of the dough sheet, then pinch the sides and tuck them underneath.

Pick up the linen and the strudel together, then roll the strudel off the linen onto the prepared baking tray, seam-side down. Brush the top with melted butter and bake for 20 minutes or until light golden.

Allow to cool, then dust generously with icing sugar, cut it into 4 pieces and serve with cream.

Visitor tips

Bars

Holy Moly →
Donaukanallände, 1010
☎ **+43 699 15 13 07 50**
badeschiff.at

The Holy Moly, a floating boat bar/ restaurant located in the heart of the 'canal district'. Food is Spanish in flavour but the menu has a bit of everything. The whole district has an air of fun and mischief, so loosen that tie and join in. In this strip alone you can view some of the best street art Vienna has to offer.

Cafes and casual eateries

Eis-Greissler →
Rotenturmstrasse 14, 1010
☎ +43 664 31 19 195
eis-greissler.at

The line out the door of this tiny ice-cream shop not far from the city centre is enormous from around 9 p.m. onwards on weekends. Not a huge range of flavours but some unusual ingredients such as goats' cheese or chocolate and pistachio balls, and frozen ice-cream truffles. All ingredients are organic, freshly churned daily with local, seasonal produce. Look out for the Eis carts dotted around the streets, and satisfy your inner child.

Meat Baby
Donaukanallände, 1010
☎ +43 800 11 11 11 11
meatbaby.at

This is a pop-up type eatery riding the current burger 'n' cocktail craze.

Milk Bar 'Meierei'
Am Heumarkt 2A, 1030 Wien
☎ +43 (1) 713 31 68
steirereck.at/meierei

A modern take on the Viennese cafe. The walk from the Sans Souci to Steidpark on a glorious morning is an easy stroll, passing palaces and grand buildings on the way, and is the best way to prepare yourself for breakfast at Milk Bar. This quirky little spot fills quickly on weekends.

If the walk has left you ravenous, order the 'Milk Bar Breakfast' for 19.90 €. It comes out on a cake stand. You may want to bring along a second stomach as this breakfast is a veritable feast, but elements such as the avocado and black olives are light and simple. Fried eggs and bacon come out with a twist: the bacon is sliced super-thin and is salty and smoky, and the chefs fry the eggs over it so it's virtually hidden.

Hotels

Hotel Palais Coburg →
Coburgbastei 4, 1010 Wien
☎ +43 1 51 81 80
palais-coburg.com
The finest hotel in Vienna, they say. Once
you are in, after a complicated admission
process involving three swipe cards, it
is pure luxury. Not modern luxury but
decadent as it comes. All suites have
mezzanine levels where the bed and
main bathroom are upstairs. The rooms
have huge ceilings; below, they all have a
small kitchenette and lounge with a great
sound system that had Australian music
downloaded on to it when the turn-down
service was completed. The menu boasts
unique dishes like hot smoked halibut or
Weiner schnitzel with classic condiments.

Restaurants

Fabio's Restaurant
Tuchlauben 6, 1010 Wien
☎ +43 15 32 22 22
fabios.at
Here, the food is what really counts, and it
is very good. Italian in theme, conventional
in menu structure, great ingredients.
I go for vitello tonnato: creamy, acidic tuna
dressing is poured over the thin poached
veal slices at the table.

The richest and most complex I have
ever tried. Beer is served in a champagne
glass, which I love – it just feels so opulent.
Squid, tomato, chilli and rigatoni is plated
perfectly. I know I'm in a real Italian
restaurant when I can count the number
of pasta shells on the plate and they equal,
both in size and number, the seafood
accompanying them.

The area itself is busy and touristy,
especially on fine evenings, so be warned
if that is not your scene. The beautiful
people of Vienna are here, watching and
being watched. The waiters love it.

Steirereck Restaurant ←
Am Heumarkt 2A, 1030 Wien
☎ +43 1 713 31 68
steirereck.at

The toilets in the basement of Steirereck, possibly Vienna's best restaurant, are without doubt the most entertaining and fun toilets I have ever had the opportunity to spend a penny in. Willy Wonka meets Bilbao museum of art on LSD.

The Bread Man wheels around an amazing trolley about half the size of the David Jones food hall with eighteen varieties of bread, my favourite being the potato and walnut closely followed by a sourdough bound with black pudding. Oh, be still my beating heart! As the waiter cleaves a loaf, steam pours from the slices. Heaven.

Another important figure is The Cheese Trolley Lady (please excuse my overuse of capitals but these appellations carry some serious heft!). Twenty-seven cheeses, half of them local. This girl is witty, confident and incredibly knowledgeable. She really knows how to entertain.

The dining room is spacious and looks out over the park and canal. The ceiling is really something: ornate plaster or lead leaf mouldings adhering to the curved ceiling with the odd halogen light recessed underneath.

Acknowledgements

To all the team at Vue de Monde for their support, hard work and great company whilst on the road, the team at Miele Australia led by Michael Jeanes, and of course Dr Markus Miele, Dr Reinhard Zinkann and Dr Heiner Olbrich, for their belief in the project. Thank you to Paula Lopez, food journalist for *El Mercurio* newspaper, for her recommendations. And big thanks to my better half for the support whilst I was on the road for many weeks at a time.

Shannon Bennett, 2014

Miele would like to thank Treasury Wines for their contribution to the Miele dinner in each country.

Index

Recipe entries are highlighted in bold.

Recipe Index

Míele

Produced for Miele by Lantern

Published by the Penguin Group
Penguin Group (Australia)
707 Collins Street, Melbourne,
Victoria 3008, Australia
(a division of Penguin Australia Pty Ltd)
Penguin Group (USA) Inc.
375 Hudson Street, New York, New York 10014, USA
Penguin Group (Canada)
90 Eglinton Avenue East, Suite 700, Toronto, Canada ON
M4P 2Y3
(a division of Penguin Canada Books Inc.)
Penguin Books Ltd
80 Strand, London WC2R 0RL England
Penguin Ireland
25 St Stephen's Green, Dublin 2, Ireland
(a division of Penguin Books Ltd)
Penguin Books India Pvt Ltd
11 Community Centre, Panchsheel Park,
New Delhi – 110 017, India
Penguin Group (NZ)
67 Apollo Drive, Rosedale, Auckland 0632,
New Zealand
(a division of Penguin New Zealand Pty Ltd)
Penguin Books (South Africa) (Pty) Ltd, Rosebank Office
Park, Block D,
181 Jan Smuts Avenue, Parktown North, Johannesburg,
2196, South Africa
Penguin (Beijing) Ltd
7F, Tower B, Jiaming Center,
27 East Third Ring Road North,
Chaoyang District, Beijing 100020, China

Penguin Books Ltd, Registered Offices:
80 Strand, London, WC2R 0RL, England

First published by Penguin Group (Australia), 2014

10 9 8 7 6 5 4 3 2 1

Text copyright © Shannon Bennett 2014

Cover and text design by Evi O © Penguin Group (Australia)
Cover photograph by Simon Griffiths
Author photograph by Simon Griffiths
Typeset in Chronicle by Post Pre-press Group, Brisbane,
Queensland
Colour separation by Splitting Image Colour Studio,
Clayton, Victoria
Printed and bound in China by 1010 Printing
International Ltd

National Library of Australia
Cataloguing-in-Publication data:

ISBN 9781921383823

Cooking all over the world/Shannon Bennett;
photography by Simon Griffiths
9781921383823 (hardback)
Includes index.
Cooking.
Voyages around the world.
Griffiths, Simon (Simon John) photographer.
641.5

penguin.com.au/lantern